Kyle teaches us that learning about mental illness makes us more Christ-like—and the reasons why shine brightly in this necessary book. In an approachable, uplifting, and relatable format, Kyle Jones offers much needed mental health education for adolescents and their parents who are navigating the challenges of today's world. In language that is easy to understand, Kyle addresses myths surrounding mental health and offers compassionate, scientific explanations for common mental health struggles like depression, anxiety, and OCD. Using stories from church history and other teens, he provides insight and encouragement for those who are struggling or love someone who is struggling with mental illness. I recommend this book to anyone who is hoping to understand mental illness through a loving, hopeful lens and wants to help shift harmful narratives about mental and emotional struggles.

—Bonnie Young
Licensed marriage and family therapist

For youth suffering with mental illness, hope is the most important resource. In this deeply sensitive and compassionate book, Kyle Bradford Jones offers hope in abundance by sharing cutting-edge knowledge, personal experience and his firm faith that "we all possess the divinity to overcome our challenges with the Savior's help." Highly recommended for any parent, family member or friend of a young person struggling to understand and heal from the growing scourge of mental illness.

—Zachary Davis
Executive Director of Faith Matters
and Editor of *Wayfare Magazine*

Dr. Jones speaks from his personal and professional experience with wit and optimism. His interviews with teenagers and other mental health experts introduce a critical basis for gospel truths that we all need to understand. These insights will help us minister to ourselves and those around us as Jesus does. This book is a must-read for all teens, anyone who knows a teen, and anyone who admits to once being a teen.

—John Bytheway

WHEN ALL HOPE SEEMS LOST

BCC
PRESS

BY COMMON CONSENT PRESS is a non-profit publisher dedicated to producing affordable, high-quality books that help define and shape the Latter-day Saint experience. BCC Press publishes books that address all aspects of Mormon life. Our mission includes finding manuscripts that will contribute to the lives of thoughtful Latter-day Saints, mentoring authors and nurturing projects to completion, and distributing important books to the Mormon audience at the lowest possible cost.

WHEN ALL HOPE SEEMS LOST

A Gospel Perspective on Mental Illness in Youth

KYLE BRADFORD JONES, MD

For information contact
By Common Consent Press
972 East Burnham Lane
Draper, Utah 84020

Cover design: Jeremy Ames
Book design: Andrew Heiss

www.bccpress.org
ISBN-13: 978-1-961471-07-8

10 9 8 7 6 5 4 3 2 1

This book is not meant as specific medical advice to any individual. Each person is different and can manifest health problems in different ways. This book is intended to be a primer, it is not meant to be comprehensive; it does not discuss every mental illness, nor does it contain every detail about the included conditions. I encourage you to reach out to your doctor for a specific evaluation or to answer your questions as needed.

This book is written from the author's perspective and experience. The opinions expressed represent those of Kyle Bradford Jones and are not necessarily those of The Church of Jesus Christ of Latter-day Saints.

Please also visit The Church of Jesus Christ of Latter-day Saints's website for mental illness to obtain several more resources: mentalhealth.churchofjesuschrist.org

Other important resources:

▷ **National Suicide and Crisis Hotline** (available 24 hours a day): 988
▷ **National Alliance on Mental Illness** (NAMI; offers support and education for individuals and families): www.nami.org
▷ **Substance Abuse and Mental Health Services Administration** (SAMHSA; provides help finding resources near you, available 24 hours a day): 1-800-662-HELP (4357)
▷ **National Institute of Mental Health** (list of various public resources): https://www.nimh.nih.gov/health/find-help/
▷ **Crisis Text Line** (crisis counseling): text HELLO to 741741

Contents

Introduction

Life is amazing sometimes. The sun shines. The birds sing. You really nail that biology test. The person you like looks your way and your heart flutters as you exchange a small smile with each other. Maybe your favorite team wins the Super Bowl, or your new best friend moves in down the street. Or you get the lead in the school play. Or you just see a hilarious meme. Yes, life can be glorious!

Life is also awful sometimes. You have a bad hair day on the night of the big party where your crush is going to be. Or a big pimple arrives on your nose overnight and no amount of washing or makeup or anything else can hide it. Sometimes it rains, or your dog gets sick, or you have to move to a new city or house. More often than not, your team doesn't even make it to the big game. Or you are dealing with bullying. Maybe you are struggling with whether you like boys or girls more, or what gender feels the most right. Or sometimes, no matter how hard you may pray or how strong your faith is, despite fasting and turning to God in complete sincerity, His answer is no and your loved one dies from cancer anyway.

We enjoy great blessings and face significant challenges all the time. The scriptures and modern-day prophets teach us that life is supposed to be a struggle to help us grow,[1] but sometimes that doesn't make it any easier. We are all called to go through challenges to become like our Heavenly Parents.[2] Of course, there are the added teenage stressors of friends, school, bullying, dating, physical changes, new hormones, worrying about embarrassing yourself in front of others, and deciding the direction you want to go in life. There are a million different decisions that seem monumental, like if you don't make the correct one, your life is ruined. And those big choices are piled on top of the everyday difficulties that life brings to all of us. It's amazing that any of us survive adolescence!

For some people, the challenges are more extreme than having a bad day, week, or month. Sometimes these challenges seem too big to cope with. Sometimes we are so nervous, so depressed, or struggling so much that the feeling interferes with our ability to manage our lives. Sometimes it's more than just feeling stress. I am, of course, talking about mental illness (though you probably guessed that since you are reading this book). A lot of things can bring it about, and there are a lot of ways the gospel of Jesus Christ supports us through our emotional struggles.

I suffer from clinical depression and anxiety. I've been on medication since 2003 and been in therapy for years. In my role as a Family Physician, I also care for people every day who have similar problems. In this book, I share some of my experiences around this to show you how important being open and honest about what we go through can help and is nothing to be embarrassed about. I hope that sharing some informa-

---

1. Moses 4:22–25; Abraham 3:24–25
2. Doctrine and Covenants 121:7–8

tion about my struggles will help put the problem in a real-life context.

Generally, a mental illness is a disorder that causes changes in your thinking, mood, feelings, physical health, and behavior. Because so many elements are impacted, there are many ways that the disorders can be organized. The majority of mental health professionals follow the *Diagnostic and Statistical Manual of Mental Disorders* (DSM) to determine a proper diagnosis.[3] The DSM is now on its fifth edition but has been around since the 1950s, with multiple updates since then. The DSM provides some concrete guidance on what the right diagnosis is when a clinical mental illness is present. It's not perfect, but it is a great tool based on the most up-to-date science that we have on these conditions. I prefer to think of the broad categories of these illnesses in a slightly different way than the DSM, though we will explore the specific diagnostic criteria for them from the DSM in the applicable chapters later on. I generally think of mental illnesses as divided into *mood disorders, anxiety disorders, and thought disorders*:[4]

1. **Mood disorders** affect, well, your mood,[5] among other things as we'll see below. Conditions such as depression or bipolar disorder are examples of mood disorders.
    a. Depression is more than just sadness, but that is obviously a large part of it. It also includes varying combinations of strong feelings of guilt, lack of energy, worthlessness, poor sleep, difficulties

---

3. Nearly all of the medical explanations described in this book come from the DSM.

4. Note that there is a lot of overlap with these categories, and the lines of some diagnoses are blurred. There are also other categories for rarer conditions, but we're gonna stick with the basics. More details of these conditions are given in the applicable chapter.

5. Shocking, I know.

concentrating, and changes in appetite. It is a very common illness among teenagers and adults.

b. Bipolar (formerly called manic-depression) is less common than depression or anxiety, but is typically more difficult to identify and treat. At least one episode each of significant depression and mania must occur for the diagnosis to be made. "Mania" is typically a combination of increased energy and great excitement, along with a need for very little sleep, racing thoughts, significant agitation, and often unsafe or impulsive behaviors. Some medications that treat depression or anxiety can bring on a manic episode if bipolar is the underlying issue, so those with bipolar need close monitoring when starting a new medication.

2. **Anxiety disorders**, such as generalized anxiety, panic attacks, social anxiety, and obsessive-compulsive disorder (OCD), are technically not mood disorders but are closely related.

a. Anxiety is a broad term that goes well beyond just feeling nervous over certain things. Anxiety often shares many of the same symptoms of depression, and can range from relatively mild to completely crippling.

b. Panic attacks are very scary events that are like an anxiety explosion that includes a racing heart, lightheadedness, extreme fear, shortness of breath, and various other symptoms. It's more than just being really anxious; it is something that momentarily cripples multiple different systems in your mind and body.

c. Social anxiety can keep you from socializing with family, friends, or peers. It often leads to isolating in your home or bedroom, and prevents you from making or maintaining meaningful relationships with others.

d. OCD often shows up as repetitive behaviors or thoughts that disrupt your life. One example is repeatedly checking if the door is locked or not. Someone with OCD may check the door multiple times, even though they know that they already checked it and it was fine. Such disruptive behaviors can cause significant problems in a teenager's life, and most of those with OCD also experience another psychiatric condition as well.

3. **Thought disorders** are conditions that lead to disorganized thinking, with or without mood problems. They include things like:

a. Schizophrenia, which is typically characterized by hallucinations—seeing or hearing things that are not really there—or severe paranoia.

b. Certain types of bipolar disorder fit better as a thought disorder, with similar symptoms as schizophrenia plus the depression and mania.[6]

Thought disorders typically appear as a young adult or late in the teenage years, while mood and anxiety disorders can appear in someone much younger. Because of this, and because mood and anxiety disorders are much more common, we'll be focusing almost exclusively on mood and anxiety disorders in this book.

---

6. Sometimes depression can have aspects of a thought disorder as well, but not very often.

Another category consideration are traumatic disorders. Prior physical, emotional, sexual, or mental trauma in your life can lead to any of the above conditions, or it can be something completely on its own. Conditions such as post-traumatic stress disorder (PTSD), attachment disorders, or adjustment disorders commonly arise from trauma. They often look like an anxiety disorder, but the main characteristic is that they keep you from adapting to different situations and relationships.[7]

Elder Alexander B. Morrison, a former member of the Quorum of the Seventy, wrote in a 2005 *Ensign* article that "increasing our understanding of mental illness helps us reach out with love and compassion to those who are suffering." In other words, *learning about mental illness helps us become more Christ-like*. Whether or not you struggle with a mental illness yourself, I guarantee you know multiple people who do.

Check out these shocking stats about how common mental illness really is:[8]

▷   Around 1 in 7 teenagers in the United States have a depressive episode per year, with even more experiencing an anxiety disorder.

▷   If you count all teenagers who will experience an episode of depression or anxiety at some point, it is closer to the adult rate of 1 in 5.

▷   Roughly 1 in every 4 people have a family member with a mental illness.

▷   Girls are much more likely to experience depression or anxiety, as are those who live in poverty.

---

7. This is yet another example of how a professional is needed to help determine a specific diagnosis.
8. All of these stats come from the National Institutes of Health.

▷ Older teenagers are more likely to experience mental illness than younger ones.

▷ A teenager dies by suicide every hour and a half in the United States.

▷ Bipolar and OCD each affect 1–3% of adolescents.

▷ Since 1999:

  ▷ Suicide is the second highest cause of death of teenagers, behind accidents.

  ▷ *Suicide has taken more teenage lives than all other known medical causes combined.*

All of these numbers have ballooned significantly in the last decade with growing concerns over the impact of social media, along with mounting social and academic pressures. However, this problem is not isolated to the United States; we see similar rates around the world, too. Even if you may not be personally struggling with an episode of mental illness, I hope this book will provide insight to better help you support others.[9]

Many teenagers attempt, or die by, suicide every year. As you can see from the statistics above, our world is devastated by the number of young people we are losing. Many kids know someone who has died by suicide. It's often difficult to predict those at highest risk of suicide and help them ease their pain. We'll take a deeper look at that later in the book.

Basically, if you have any of these extreme symptoms in your life, you are not alone—you are actually among millions of others around the world. You should not expect to overcome it on your own, because no one can alone. Effectively addressing mental illness is a team sport.

Given these growing numbers and impact of mental illness on our spirituality, the leaders of The Church of Jesus Christ of

---

9. Mosiah 2:17; Matthew 25:40; Doctrine and Covenants 81:5

Latter-day Saints have given mental health increasing attention in recent years.[10] However, negative stigma and misunderstanding by many members of the church continue. Many people still consider mental illness to be a moral failing, or a lack of faith, or something that improves merely with positive thinking. These myths do more harm than good, especially as we are developing physically, emotionally, and spiritually in our teenage years. It is critical for all of us to understand that *there is no reason to feel ashamed if we have a mental illness*, just as there is no shame in having any other disease; it is not the individual's fault. But failing to address the issue can lead to a lifetime of further struggles. **But there is always hope in Jesus Christ. Why? *Because He loves us.***[11] (We will have a few different "broken records" in this book; this is **Broken Record #1.**)[12] He overcame the world,[13] and is the only One in whom we can have complete hope.[14] We have multiple tools available to help us with any mental or emotional struggles we experience, and through Jesus's sacrifice, there is always hope of functioning and thriving in our damaged world.

Elder Jeffrey R. Holland spoke about mental illness in General Conference in 2013. I would encourage all of you to read his talk "Like a Broken Vessel," which is filled with much wisdom. He clarified the difference between everyday struggles and mental illness:

---

10. Check out mentalhealth.churchofjesuschrist.org for lots of church info and resources.

11. John 3:16; Alma 24:14

12. Have you ever seen a record? If you haven't, just ask your hipster uncle. A "broken record" just keeps repeating itself. Hence, the most important concepts in this book will be repeated over and over and over like a broken record. Pay special attention to these!

13. John 16:33

14. Moroni 7:41; Joel 3:16

> When I speak of [depression], I am not speaking
> of bad hair days, tax deadlines, or other discour-
> aging moments we all have. Everyone is going to
> be anxious or downhearted on occasion. The Book
> of Mormon says Ammon and his brethren were
> depressed at a very difficult time, and so can the
> rest of us be. But today I am speaking of some-
> thing more serious, of an affliction so severe that
> it significantly restricts a person's ability to func-
> tion fully, a crater in the mind so deep that no one
> can responsibly suggest it would surely go away
> if those victims would just square their shoulders
> and think more positively.

I hope this book is not too (ahem) depressing, because this can be a hard topic to read and talk about. My intent is not to drag us all down into further depths by dwelling on negative things. The idea is to educate us all about the realities of clinical mental illness, how we can distinguish it from our typical interactions with life, and to provide some direction toward what we can do about it. Importantly, you need to understand that *there is no shame in having a mental illness* (**Broken Record #2**). It is *not your fault*, nor is it a moral failing or sign of poor character. It does *not* make you a failure or a bad person. One of the therapists you'll meet later in the book said, "Sometimes it's not your choice, it's your chemistry."

Mental illness is very common for individuals who are struggling with their sexuality, gender identity, or various marginalized identities. The LGBTQ+ community experiences depression, anxiety, and substance abuse disorders at a rate two-and-a-half times more than the general population, largely as a result from the negative response they receive from loved ones and society. They are *almost five times more likely to attempt suicide*. This can be an extremely difficult challenge. Broken Record #1 applies to all of us, no matter what.

God loves all of us, and so should we. We won't discuss specific LGBTQ+ issues beyond emotional difficulties in this book, not because it isn't important, but more because it is not the primary focus here. However, the general principles we talk about apply to everyone.

Elder Alexander B. Morrison, in his great book on mental illness *Valley of Sorrow*, wonderfully said when dispelling popular myths about mental illness,

> Most often, lacking an understanding about the causes of mental illness, victims blame *themselves*, and may seem unable to rid themselves of terrible though undefined feelings that somehow, some way *they* are the cause of their own pain—even when they're not. Parents, spouses, or other family members of mentally ill persons too often needlessly harrow up their own minds, trying futilely to determine where *they* went wrong. They pray repeatedly for forgiveness, when there is no evidence they have anything of note for which to repent. They may try to bargain with God, offering Him anything, even their own lives, if only He will 'cure' their beloved child or family member. Of course, in the vast majority of instances none of this works, simply because the victim's thoughts and behavior result from disease processes, which are not caused by the actions of others, including God. (Italics in original)

Having a mental illness doesn't mean that you just need to read your scriptures more, or that having more faith will make it go away. It is a physical disease like any other, such as cancer or diabetes. Unlike many other illnesses, we cannot diagnose a mental illness with a blood test or x-ray. It is invisible and can be much harder to discover and much easier to hide. However, like other diseases, there is treatment and help available if we're willing to accept it.

Throughout the book, I include some thoughts and advice from multiple mental health professionals and experts who know more about this than I do. I also share some stories from teenagers *just like you*. I am obviously not a teenager (though I always picture myself in just as good of shape as I was in high school), so I am learning from many of you what it's like to be an adolescent in today's world. The world you face differs greatly from the one I and your parents faced as a teenager, and it brings unique challenges. The inspiration given to ancient and modern-day prophets also has much to contribute to our discussion.

While parents, guardians, and other care takers can be a pain in the neck sometimes, they definitely love you and want to support you in your physical and spiritual progression as much as possible.[15] There is a special section near the end of the book for your parents to provide them with some ideas about how to help you. But you know better than I do what advice to give them, so please discuss the advice with your parents and family so they can better help *you*. I would encourage you to read the chapter for parents so you can adapt the advice given to your own family interactions and relationships.

The most important thing for you to remember, both while reading this and after you're done, is that **Jesus loves you.**[16] He is aware of your struggles, no matter how severe they may be. He has been through them Himself and knows how

---

15. I recognize that there are exceptions to this. Some parents are abusive or neglectful, and I so hope that such a situation does not apply to you. The wonderful thing is that we all have our Heavenly Parents who do love us and want the best for us.

16. Broken Record #1!

to comfort you.[17] When weighed down with such debilitating illnesses, we need to make use of all of God's gifts to do the best we can, which include medications, therapy, or any other medical treatments your doctor recommends. Prayer, blessings, and fasting are important when we have any illness, but they are typically not enough by themselves.

As part of his General Conference talk mentioned above, Elder Holland added "If you had appendicitis, God would expect you to seek a priesthood blessing and get the best medical care available. So too with emotional disorders. Our Father in Heaven expects us to use all of the marvelous gifts He has provided in this glorious dispensation."

Elder Dale G. Renlund shared this thought at a BYU devotional in December 2019:

> Clinical anxiety and depression require professional help. God expects us to seek professional help when indicated. Remember Captain Moroni's rhetorically sarcastic response to Pahoran: 'Or do ye suppose that the Lord will still deliver us while . . . we do not make use of the means which the Lord has provided for us?' Prayers in this situation may seem somewhat insincere to God as they're manifestations of faith without works.

Mental illness is not something that goes away with just positive thinking, or just pills, or just exercise alone, but these and other efforts are often necessary to treat it. It takes work, just like managing any disease does, but *we all possess the divinity to overcome our challenges with the Savior's help.* Given our current understanding of mental illness, we know it can be managed, and sometimes eliminated. Some people surmount it completely, and it only lasts a relatively short time,

---

17. Alma 7:11–12; John 14:16–18.

and some people carry it with them forever (though it can be treated). I still have times of extreme depression and anxiety, but most of the time, I do just fine. It's a bit like a dog on a leash—I am mostly in control, though every once in a while, Fido yanks me in a certain direction when he sees something he wants. I still use medication daily and meet with my therapist, but I also control the dog on the leash. My life is great most of the time.

If you struggle, work with your family, your doctor, trusted friends, and others who can offer you support. Allow yourself to feel tough emotions because life isn't about eliminating the bad but knowing how to deal with it. God won't give us more than we can handle.[18] There are blessings that come when we follow our Savior Jesus Christ, regardless of whether we recognize them. You have no less worth in God's eyes if you have a mental illness; He is not ashamed of you if you do. You are still a divine child of the Almighty God of the universe. *No matter how hard things are, there is always hope in Jesus!*[19]

---

18. 1 Corinthians 10:13; 1 Nephi 3:7
19. Broken Record #1 strikes again!

CHAPTER ONE

How Do I Know if I Have a Mental Illness and What to do About It

Now we get into some of the tough stuff. How do we know whether we have a mental illness, or even which one, when we are struggling in life?

I'll use both depression and anxiety as the main examples, as they are two of the most common. Depression and anxiety are *normal emotions* that everyone experiences from time to time (**Broken Record #3**). Not only are they normal emotions, but they are *essential* emotions—we couldn't progress as our Heavenly Father wants us to without them.[1] Adam and Eve were taught that if they didn't know suffering and pain, then

---

1. 2 Nephi 2:11

they would never know joy.² Sometimes that doesn't offer any solace, but it is comforting to know that no matter who you are, we *all* struggle with difficulties, even the popular kid at school that seems a little too perfect.

It's appropriate to be nervous before a big test or presentation coming up. In fact, it can even be motivation to prepare and do our best. We may feel depressed when something bad happens, but it can help to guide us and our decision-making in the future. It also helps us appreciate the joy all the more when it comes.

Depression and anxiety can also be a *symptom* of some diseases. Imbalances of hormones, such as those involved in thyroid disease or some cancers, can cause us to feel these emotions when we otherwise wouldn't. Side effects of certain medications can also mimic mental illness. Thus, the presence of depression or anxiety can sometimes serve as a warning of something else going on. Your doctor can evaluate you for some of these causes by asking a lot of questions and doing an exam. And a medical professional may choose to draw some blood or do other tests to rule out other conditions.

But depression and anxiety can also be a clinical *diagnosis* when either one gets really out of hand. A diagnosis is confirmation that you have a mental illness, like millions of others, including myself. It's difficult to distinguish among these three aspects of depression and anxiety: emotion, symptom, or diagnosis. There is no blood test, no scan of your brain, no bright neon light flashing over our head to help us diagnose it. There also isn't a perfect continuum upon which we can say, "Yesterday you were experiencing something normal, but today it's a disease." It's like having a robot butler that one day

---

2. Moses 5:11

turns on you.[3] The robot is nice to have (like our normal emotions), but when it goes bad and tries to harm us and our family (like a mental illness), everything changes. What caused it to cross that line? I don't know, but we explore some possibilities below. However, we do have some guidance to help us distinguish between the emotions and diagnoses of depression and anxiety.

The biggest difference between a mental illness and experiencing appropriate emotion is that the former completely disrupts your life. This can occur either because it becomes overly bothersome to you, or because it keeps you from functioning the way you had before. I've had many times when I became severely anxious for no reason and it kept me from doing things that I enjoy. My depression has completely sabotaged my ability to function physically or mentally for days at a time. It almost seems like an outside entity invades your spirit and body, trying to keep you from accomplishing what you need and want to.

Clinical depression and anxiety also include other symptoms beyond just extreme emotion. Clinical depression is *not just feeling sad*; there are other signs that go along with it, such as guilt, poor concentration, feelings of worthlessness, decreased energy, and others.[4] It's the same with anxiety. An anxiety disorder is more than being anxious all the time. It can disrupt your sleep, your appetite, your thinking, concentration, or memory, and include other problems, such as headaches. A mental illness diagnosis is much more than just excess emotion.

We often need to distinguish between *primary depression or anxiety* and *secondary depression or anxiety*. A primary, or

3. Stupid analogy, you say? I disagree. You wouldn't say that if *you* had a robot butler turn on you!
4. We'll go more in depth later in the book.

biological, mental illness typically has a genetic cause. If one of your parents or siblings has a mental illness, then you are more likely to have one. That doesn't guarantee you'll *experience* a mental illness, just that your risk is higher. Sometimes a specific event may trigger the illness inside of you, but it is more related to your genes than the event.

A secondary, or situational, mental illness typically comes from a specific event or problem that can go away. Sometimes there is an event in your life that may bring on a diagnosable mental illness for a relatively short time, which resolves when you take away the stressor. For example, it is common to become severely depressed when a loved one is having a significant health crisis. Individuals and their loved ones who have cancer, as an example, are much more likely to develop depression. However, if that disease is cured or brought under good control, the depression often goes away. Another example is bullying in school. It can cause such stress and trauma that an individual can meet criteria for a clinical mental illness, but once the bullying stops, the symptoms can completely resolve. It's like dumping gasoline on a fire—it makes the fire roar much bigger, but the gas eventually is consumed and the fire calmed. A primary mental illness, on the other hand, may remain after the specific stressor resolves (after the gasoline has burned away), but it also doesn't mean that it will last your entire life.

Secondary depression or anxiety is sometimes more appropriately diagnosed as an *adjustment disorder*. An adjustment disorder is a more profound response to a specific stressor than we would otherwise expect. For example, it would be normal for you to grieve the death of your pet, but we wouldn't expect it to shut down your life for months on end. An adjustment disorder can manifest with anxiety, depression, behavioral problems, or any combination of those three. These symptoms typically last less than six months but can last longer.

Kelly Furr, a Marriage and Family Therapist from Arizona, says that she sees more teens with adjustment disorder than clinical depression or anxiety. Big changes in life can be more difficult on teenagers and children, she explains, because "they don't have as much autonomy to change their situation as adults do. They have less power to get themselves out of a circumstance that isn't helpful." In short, teenagers don't have as much control over their lives as a typical adult would, and thus even changes that seem small can cause a significant disruption in their well-being.[5]

An adjustment disorder can mimic multiple other mental illnesses, and there are often a lot of similarities to things like depression, anxiety, OCD, and bipolar. So how do we tell the difference? Physicians and psychologists[6] regularly use the DSM, that we discussed in the Introduction, to determine a proper diagnosis.[7] There are some other diagnostic questionnaires and tests that your doctor or therapist may deem fit to use. Sometimes there is some uncertainty of which illness may be most present, or if there are other things that are complicating your condition, such as some sort of mental disability, and so further testing may be needed. Your doctor and therapist can help guide you to what evaluation is most relevant to you.

---

5. Alma teaches us how impactful even small things can be—Alma 37:6.

6. Psychologists have a PhD, a nonmedical degree, and thus are unable to prescribe medication. However, they are a critical member of the healthcare team. They are often confused with psychiatrists, doctors who have the ability to prescribe medication, though primary care doctors also treat many mental illnesses. There are also other professionals who can conduct therapy with you, particularly social workers.

7. Do you remember this? It's the "bible" for diagnosing mental illness. We'll keep seeing it throughout the book.

Sometimes a mental illness shows up with mainly physical symptoms. For example, I was not diagnosed with generalized anxiety disorder until after I had years of stomach troubles with diarrhea (called irritable bowel syndrome), something which is common with extreme anxiety. I also had a panic attack, what I described as an "anxiety explosion" in the Introduction.[8] I thought I was having heart problems when my doctor told me it was anxiety. Other common physical symptoms caused by mental illnesses can include headaches, being exhausted or not tired at all, any sort of stomach upset (especially for younger kids), or worsening of any existing pain. Often these symptoms may appear at a time of anticipated stressors, such as a stomachache to avoid going to school where you are being bullied. But they can also come out of nowhere, too.

Sometimes adolescents show their mental illness in different ways than adults do. Any significant change from one's baseline, or typical behavior, can be an early sign of difficulty. Adults are often better able to hide their feelings with their behavior than a teenager who has a still-developing brain and body. Lisa Gauchay, a therapist who works with families at the Huntsman Cancer Institute in Salt Lake City, Utah, points out how changes in concentration can also affect teenagers more than adults: "Change in attention span is a really important thing to look at. I think we're quick to diagnose ADHD[9] when sometimes it's a depression issue. Kids notice that because they have to do a lot of concentrating with school, and adults can kind of slide by that sometimes." Kelly Furr, the therapist from Arizona mentioned before, describes how "teenagers are more likely to self-harm. They are more likely to do some impulsive behaviors, like teenagers are inclined to do. They may

---

8. Thankfully you don't *actually* explode, but it kinda feels like you might.
9. Attention deficit hyperactivity disorder, a common disease that affects focus and concentration.

be less likely to think through things that might hurt them." It doesn't mean that adults never show these signs, but teenagers may be more likely to show these behaviors than others.

Sorting through these factors to determine if you have a mental illness can be very difficult. Because there are so many elements to determine what you are experiencing, it is important that you *do not diagnose yourself (or others) without professional help*. Just as you would seek medical input for any other physical symptoms, you should do this for any mental or emotional symptoms as well. This may sound like a silly thing, but it can actually be a big problem for some people.

Impact of a Mental Illness

There are many potential ramifications of mental illness on your physical health, relationships, spirituality, school, and work. It is absolutely critical that you seek appropriate treatment so that the mental illness doesn't sink you.

1. **Physical Diseases**   We already talked about how certain diseases can cause depressed or anxious moods, but there are also some diseases that a mental illness worsens. Depression and anxiety increase the stress hormones in your body which, over time, wear down your heart and kidneys, can cause weight gain, increase your blood pressure, give you diabetes, and literally[10] change the structure of your brain! There is some research suggesting that you are more likely to develop dementia if you have an untreated mental illness. People with unaddressed, serious anxiety are more likely to experience a heart attack later in life. I know much of this doesn't seem too serious because it

---

10. I don't mean the pretend "literally" that literally everyone says, I mean *actually literally!*

may not affect you for years, but it'll catch up with you. These stress hormones also weaken your immune system and can cause chronic inflammation, so you are likely to get sick more often. Any wound, such as a scrape, cut, or even a pimple, heals more slowly with elevated levels of these hormones.[11]

2. **Relationships** Your relationship with others is often what's most profoundly affected by mental illness. Those with depression, anxiety, obsessive-compulsive disorder (OCD), bipolar, and other illnesses commonly avoid social interactions. Isolation, both physically and emotionally, from others is a natural response to mental difficulties but can also worsen them. Many have the tendency in this situation to avoid talking to their parents or other family members, with friends, or anyone else. Even the more you use your phone and less you interact with people in-person, the more isolated you actually become. Teenagers who suffer from mental illness are less likely to go on dates, hang out with friends, or even have close friends. This lack of connection leads to further self-imposed isolation, which worsens mood and ability to cope with problems.

3. **Spirituality** The most important relationship that can be damaged is that with our Heavenly Father. Being in the throes of depression or other illness can make it extremely difficult to feel the Spirit. The Spirit is the main way we connect with our Heavenly Father, and not feeling that connection leads to further issues. We often think that it is our fault that we cannot connect, that God is mad at us,

---

11. Did I just imply that severe anxiety can worsen your acne? Yes, yes I did.

or that He isn't real or doesn't love us.[12] Our testimonies may suffer and our spiritual progress be impeded, but you can work through this challenge. We'll explore this more in the next chapter, but it is important to recognize that having a mental illness can damage our spirit as much as it can our physical body and mind. This disconnect from God has more negative ramifications than any other from mental illness. Our mental and emotional struggles do not come from our relationship with God. Just because you are struggling does not mean that you don't love God, or that He doesn't love you.

4. **School and Work**   It is very common for one's grades, school activities, and job performance to worsen because of a mental illness. It's often harder to concentrate, tougher to find the motivation to study or do homework,[13] and more difficult to even go to school or work sometimes. Mental illness can really set you on a negative path for your future. However, your school has some resources to support your learning in the setting of a mental illness to make sure you don't fall behind; take advantage of this.

Treatment

Regine Galanti, PhD, a clinical psychologist who practices in New York and author of *Anxiety Relief for Teens*, describes our emotions as having three parts: our thoughts, physical feelings, and our behaviors. These all interact together to frame how we experience our emotions. There are other spiritual and physical components that affect our mental and emotional function, too. So, what are some treatments? Because there are so

---

12. Remember Broken Record #1? He *always* loves you.
13. Well, worse than usual, anyway.

many elements to our mental health, we need to approach our emotional well-being in multiple different ways. We need to address our thoughts and feelings, behaviors and habits, and physical and spiritual health. We'll discuss some of the spiritual approaches in the next chapter, but here are some things that are scientifically shown to help our mental well-being:

1. **Exercise** Consistent cardiovascular exercise, such as running, bicycling, or other intense activities, can raise levels of positive chemicals in your brain. It also helps your body to be as healthy as possible, which can decrease the impact of other diseases which may negatively affect your life. The activity should raise your heart rate enough that it is tough to speak without pausing to breathe. Experts recommend at least 150 minutes of such exercise each week. This goes along with eating a lot of protein, fruits, and vegetables, and drinking a lot of water and very few sugary drinks like soda or juice. You can still enjoy soda or treats sometimes, but overdoing it on junk food gets us feeling worse about ourselves and life.

2. **Sleep** Without enough sleep, our bodies struggle to regulate mental and physical health. In my medical practice, we focus on getting good sleep before working on anything else to address mood problems. Luckily enough, exercise is one way to improve your sleep. Sometimes all it takes is focusing on *sleep hygiene*,[14] and sometimes you may need some medication to help. And sometimes you just need to put your phone away![15]

---

14. "Sleep hygiene" are behavioral and environmental things that help prepare your body for sleep. Examples include sleeping in a quiet, dark room that's not too hot or cold; avoiding the use of screens for at least one hour before bedtime; having a consistent sleep routine; etc.

15. I'm sorry, but it's true.

3. **Behaviors**   Our behavior can have a serious impact on our mental health. There are a lot of studies that show a connection between depression, anxiety, and social media use among teenagers. Limiting our time on popular social media sites helps us decrease the effects of cyber-bullying, feelings of inadequacy from comparing ourselves to others, inappropriate online relationships, hateful speech, and damaging relationships. Beyond social media, even using any sort of screen for a long period—whether watching television, playing video games, or using a computer—can negatively affect your mental health.[16] If you're like my kids, you're tired of your parents nagging at you to get off of your screen, but it really does help. Too much screen use can also negatively influence your grades and other activities that you might pursue. Focusing more on positive in-person interactions helps our sense of well-being. So, the next time you're with your family or friends or basically *anyone*, put your phone down and talk to them.[17] I promise it will help both of you!

4. **Therapy**   There are many types of "talk therapy" that work, but there is a big misconception about what therapy actually is. It's not merely your health insurance or parents paying some stranger to listen to your problems (or not listen, if you won't tell them anything). It's more than simply having someone to talk to, though that is part of it. Your therapist can help guide you to restructure how you think and approach the difficulties you are facing. Cognitive-behavioral therapy (CBT) is the most common, but other types exist. The process is very similar to working with a coach in sports. The coach teaches you, offers encouragement,

---

16. I'm sorry, but it's true.
17. I'm sorry, but it's true.

and is invested in your success, just like your therapist will be. You and your therapist can work together to figure out what is best for you depending on your specific diagnosis, your goals of therapy, and how willing you are to work on the direction your therapist provides you. Your therapist may recommend group therapies, where other people with similar struggles and needs can support each other in their treatment. Therapy with you and your family can also be very helpful to improve the way you all communicate with each other. There are even some formal art and music therapies that may be helpful in certain circumstances.

5. **Support groups**   Think of support groups as informal therapy. These are primarily for those with a mental illness, or their loved ones, and include people in similar situations to connect and offer support to each other. Many people find these groups to be very helpful, whether they're in-person events, conducted over social media, or through video conferencing. Groups can be important to help you feel that you are not alone, especially when mental illness can be so isolating.

6. **Medication**   Studies show that the best outcomes for many with mental illness are a combination of therapy and medication, along with the behaviors mentioned above. There are many medications that can treat mental illness, but it depends upon your diagnosis and your specific symptoms. Work with your doctor to figure out which medicine best suits you, if you need it. If there is a medication that has worked well for a family member of yours, then it is more likely to work well for you. Medications won't completely take away all of your bad feelings, but they can help—*a lot*. I will tell you about some common medications used for each diagnosis in an Extra Credit section later on.

Whenever Victoria Hatton, a high school psychologist, has a student or parent come to her with a question about how to help a teenager, she always tells them to start with their physical health. "If for two weeks, your child is going to bed and waking up at the same time, you're making sure that they're getting all the nutrients they need, and they're doing at least 20 minutes of exercise every day, and [their struggles] are still there, then let's talk. But if it goes away with those things, then it's probably normal adolescent stuff."[18]

If you have a mental illness, it's possible that you may need to stay in the hospital for a short time, depending on how severe your symptoms are. This most often happens to those who want to harm themselves or even take their own life. A hospital stay isn't failure—it's setting you on a better path toward feeling good and accomplishing what you want in life. It's to help you get back to yourself, because you are someone pretty special! Your personal worth does not diminish if you stay in the hospital because of your mental illness.[19] But not getting treatment is like preparing your body and spirit to implode, like a building being demolished.

Many people worry that if they see a therapist or doctor, other people will find out. Therapists and doctors are ethically and legally bound to keep your information private. I saw a patient once who was in his early 20s and refused medication because he was convinced his employer would find out and fire him. This man truly needed medication, but I couldn't convince him it was not his employer's business if he took medication or not. There are also multiple laws in the United States and many other countries to protect people from being fired for having specific illnesses or disabilities.

---

18. Yes, this *does* mean eating your vegetables. I know you can do it!
19. Broken Record #2!

Ironically enough, this guy was probably more likely to be fired for *not* taking medication and working while severely depressed than by taking medications. When we neglect or ignore a serious problem, it only gets worse and we tend to engage in dangerous behaviors. This can include abusing alcohol or taking drugs. People with untreated mental illness are more likely to have unprotected sex with multiple partners or turn to illegal behavior, such as stealing and violence towards others. Most people with an untreated mental illness obviously don't act this way, but we are at a higher risk of doing so. As a teenager, with your body and mind still developing, you are also more likely to behave impulsively, without thinking through all the potential consequences of your actions.[20] Again, this doesn't mean that a teenager who doesn't treat their mental illness is definitely going to do something stupid, but your chances are higher than otherwise. Treating any mental illness affects every part of our life!

I also fully recognize that substantial barriers often exist to getting treatment. Sometimes there simply aren't any therapists or doctors in your area that can help, or they have a long waiting list. Other times, it may cost too much money, either because you don't have health insurance, or the insurance that you have requires you to pay a lot of money to get these services. Even if there is someone in your area who can treat you and money isn't an obstacle, health care is just complicated. No matter how smart you are, sometimes the system is simply too confusing to navigate easily. Or maybe you want some help from a therapist or doctor, but your loved ones disagree and won't support your efforts. These are really hard things to manage, and some people give up trying to get help when fac-

---

20. I don't want you to feel like I'm picking on teenagers. Every person is different, but the way that our brains and bodies develop make us more impulsive in our teenage years than at other times in life.

ing these barriers. Your bishop or other church leaders cannot (and should not) fill the role of your therapist or physician, but they can help connect you with church or community resources to get you the support you need. Don't let these added obstacles (or others that I didn't mention) keep you from getting help.

COMMON QUESTION

▶ **My brother told me that I'm just crazy and that's why I feel so depressed. Am I going crazy?**

◁ No. "Crazy" is a very charged word that people often mistakenly associate with any emotional or mental struggle. You're not crazy even though you may have a mental illness.

▶ **Are you sure?**

◁ Yes, I am.

▶ **How do you know?**

◁ Because I'm a doctor. And I've experienced those feelings too. Don't worry—you're not crazy or insane or nuts or bonkers or cuckoo or loony or psycho or deranged or imbalanced (should I keep going?); you just have something to work through that many other people don't have or understand.

How the Brain Regulates Your Mood

There are a couple of extra credit sections in this book. They contain additional information about mental illness that can be helpful to understand the various diseases but are unnecessary to comprehend the core message of this book—which is that there is no shame in having a mental illness and that Jesus loves you no matter what.

As mentioned above, depression, anxiety, bipolar, or any other mental illness is a physical disease like many others. Some areas of the brain are overactive or underactive in certain people. For example, the amygdala, an area of the brain that helps control our emotional responses (especially fear and anxiety), tends to be bigger than average in those with anxiety disorders. Whether the person has anxiety because the amygdala is bigger, or the amygdala is bigger because one has more anxiety, isn't always clear; it can probably go either way.

It's not just the size of the different areas of the brain, but more importantly, how the communication within the brain occurs. Throughout our body, there is a complex working of chemicals, hormones, enzymes, and other things that regulate how our bodies work. Such elements control things such as our heart function, breathing, appetite, etc., all the way down to precisely how much potassium is in our blood. Many such chemicals in our brains are called *neurotransmitters*. Neurotransmitters help the neurons, or cells, in our brain communicate with one another to run our body. They all do different things, but three specific neurotransmitters—serotonin, norepinephrine, and dopamine—interact within our brain to impact our mood.

▷ **Serotonin**   This chemical helps regulate anxiety, creation of certain memories, our various impulses, etc.
▷ **Norepinephrine**   This chemical has to do with concentration, energy, and attention.
▷ **Dopamine**   This chemical plays a big role in excitement, motivation, and clear thinking.

As you can see in the diagram below, these three neurotransmitters work together to affect our mood and much of our behavior. Many common medications for various mental illnesses address the levels of one or more of these chemicals. But, as you could guess, there is a delicate balance between all of them to help us properly function in life. Their function and levels are highly related to genetics (i.e., if you have a family member with a specific mental illness, you have a higher likelihood of getting it yourself, but *not* a guarantee), stressful things in life, or history of a traumatic event (like suffering abuse or seeing a loved one die). They are also related to our physical health and other things in our environment, such as social media use, drug or alcohol abuse, our diet, and even the weather. Some of these things we can control, but not all of them.[1] And sometimes we can do everything in our power to optimize the above influences, and we *still* have problems. This is where the neurotransmitters fit in. If the areas of our brain cannot communicate with each other, we simply do not function well.

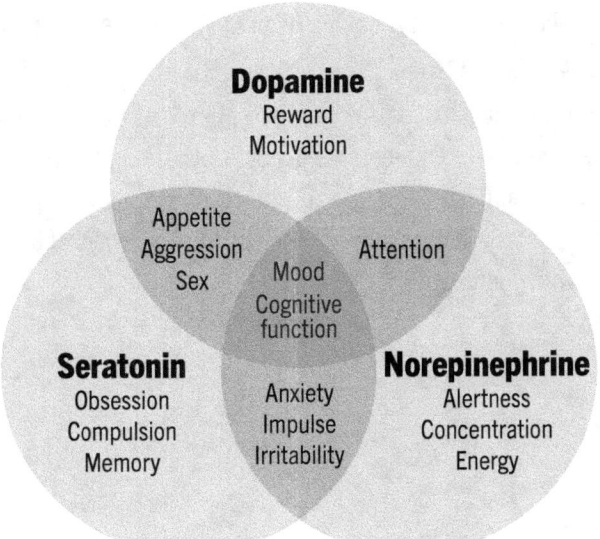

Admittedly, ***this isn't the complete story*** of the origins of mental illness. We don't have all the answers for how these or other chemicals work together to control our mood. We have a general understanding, but many of the details elude us. There are doubtless many other things in our lives that contribute to our mental well-being. We are the sum of so many things,

---

1. Wouldn't it be so cool to control the weather?!

both temporal and spiritual, mental and physical, internal and external. There are many more aspects to this illness than we currently recognize, and there is rarely a single cause of an individual's mental illness.

COMMON QUESTION

▶ My teacher said that my grades are bad because I'm lazy, but I really can't concentrate in class. I try really hard. I don't sleep the night before a test, I get so nervous that I can't remember anything I study. My heart pounds, it's hard to breathe, and it feels like the world is caving in on me when I get to the test. Is my teacher right?

◁ No. Your problem isn't from laziness, but is related to a severe anxiety surrounding tests (and maybe other things). This is very common among teens. Talk to your teachers to let them know. Your school will have some resources or other ways of helping you with your learning.

CHAPTER TWO

Mental Illness and the Gospel

Jesus preached the Sermon on the Mount as recorded in Matthew chapters 5–7, and shared very similar thoughts on the American continent after His resurrection in the Book of Mormon, starting in 3 Nephi, chapter 11. He says in that sermon to the Nephites, "Therefore I would that ye should be perfect even as I, or your Father who is in heaven is perfect."[1] This notion has caused many believers a lot of distress. Many of us who are members of The Church of Jesus Christ of Latter-day Saints strive for perfect obedience—we want to do the best we can to fulfill all the commandments, thus becoming perfect. But there are two problems in our typical interpretation of this scripture. First, we cannot fulfill this

---

1. 3 Nephi 12:48

commandment while on earth; it is an impossible task both in our current mortal state and without the atonement of Jesus Christ. We can eventually be perfected through Christ based on our faithfulness and His grace, and making and keeping sacred ordinances like baptism and those in the temple, but our road to perfection includes constant repentance and relying upon Jesus. Repentance isn't a bad or scary thing! It's actually a wonderful thing that allows us to progress. Second, the scriptural meaning of perfection is *completeness*, as opposed to our cultural meaning of the word as *without flaw*.

So why do I bring this up in a book about mental illness? The notion of perfection in *this* life on earth comes from a *cultural* interpretation of the scriptures, but it is *not* a doctrine of the gospel of Jesus Christ. Ours is an eternal journey that began before this life and continues well after death. Many of us get caught up in *perfectionism*, or severe self-criticism for our weaknesses, believing that we are not as good as we think we should be. The Savior taught us that we need to "continue in patience until [we] are perfected."[2] This tells us two things: 1) Perfection does not occur quickly. We need to remember that Jesus was not perfected until after His resurrection, and we have a *long* way to go to reach that end. 2) We do not perfect ourselves, but it comes from Christ. *He* perfects *us*. We are *striving to be worthy*, which isn't the same as perfection. Elder Cecil O. Samuelson described it like this:

> Occasionally, for well-motivated and highly devoted Latter-day Saints, confusion occurs about the differences between worthiness and perfection. Worthiness and perfection don't mean the same thing! [. . .] Be sure that you do not have higher standards for yourself or others than the Lord has

---

2. Doctrine and Covenants 67:13

established. These good people suffer from exaggerating their minor mistakes, weaknesses, or shortcomings to the point that they may become dysfunctional.[3]

He later quotes then-Elder Russell M. Nelson: "We all need to remember: men are that they might have joy—not guilt trips!"

The folly of perfectionism is common within many religious communities. Not only do we assume we shouldn't make mistakes, but we also want to make sure that no one else sees any of those mistakes. Our seemingly fault-free lives then lead others to think that they are not good enough because they aren't as righteous or blessed or wealthy or good looking or, well, as perfect, as we are. And then we get the same message from them. And around it goes.

Perfectionism often leads to significant anxiety and depression among those who accept this premise that they don't measure up to others. Many even leave their church or lose their testimony because of these false notions. Some end up needing more intense treatment for mental illness. This view of perfection is based on *fear*, whereas the perfection through Christ's atonement is based on *love*. As I've said (and I'll keep saying!), it's okay to struggle, and you don't need to attack yourself needlessly for being different from others.

You can probably guess what my thoughts are about this topic since you've read this far. While it can be an easy trap to fall into, I think that comparing ourselves to others and trying to be "more perfect" than they are is self-destructive, and very little positive can come of it. Yet, it's such an easy trap to fall into! It's human nature to think this way. This is also where many of the negative effects of social media come

---

3. "What does it mean to be perfect?" *New Era*, January 2006.

in. We might have a voice telling us that, for example, because I didn't get as many likes, I'm not as beautiful, I don't have as big of muscles, that party I wasn't invited to looks really fun, or I just don't own as nice of clothes—and so I am not worth as much as someone else is. It's simply not true. Don't beat yourself up! We all have our own unique talents that differ from others. You are *still* a child of the Almighty God, the greatest Being in all the universe! That's pretty cool. And He doesn't expect you to be perfect right now: He expects you to keep repenting so that the atonement of Jesus Christ can bring you closer to Him.

Adversity and struggles are part of living on earth. We absolutely, without a doubt, one hundred percent *will* experience tough things in life. Sometimes our misfortunes result from our choices, or from other's choices, and sometimes they just happen. No matter what struggles you face, you cannot become like our Heavenly Parents and the Savior Jesus Christ without them. The prophet Lehi taught his kids that "it must needs be, that there is an opposition in all things."[4] If we don't know sorrow, we cannot know joy and happiness. If we do not know sickness, we cannot know health. I would never wish depression or anxiety or other mental and emotional difficulties on anyone, but its presence may be part of our personal life experience *to bring us closer to God*. That's especially tough to accept when you are in the middle of it, and you may think that God hates you for allowing you to carry this burden, but that is never true. *God never hates you.*

And yet it can be *so* hard to feel the Spirit when you are in the middle of the darkness of a mental illness. The negative effects on our brains and bodies from these diseases can dull our spirit and its ability to interact with the Spirit of the Lord.

---

4. 2 Nephi 2:11

Many people feel trapped, or even abandoned by the Lord, when this happens. Questions arise: What did I do wrong? Why am I going through this? Does God even exist? And if He does exist, does He even care that I am dealing with this?

Small but significant signs still exist of God's love, no matter what.[5] That you have people who love you and want to help you is a gift from God. The scientific advances that we have in different therapies and medications are inspired by God. God has not abandoned you, and He *definitely* loves you more than you know. If you look for signs from God, even small ones, that He loves you, then I promise you will find them.

It's also easy to believe that it must be our fault that the Spirit isn't present more often. The scriptures continuously talk about losing the Spirit when we are unrighteous.[6] It is therefore easy to assume that since you cannot feel the Spirit, it must be because you sinned. This is not necessarily true! Going back to Elder Renlund's BYU devotional that I referenced in the introduction, he said, "The inability to sense God's love can stem from sin, or from not pressing forward on the covenant path. *The inability can also be due to physical or mental illness*" (emphasis mine). There are many ways to communicate with the Spirit, and also many barriers that keep us away from Its influence.

One of the best examples of the folly of perfectionism and mental illness in the history of The Church of Jesus Christ of Latter-day Saints is the story of former church President George Albert Smith. He was considered one of the kindest, gentlest, and most charitable men that you might ever meet. But beneath his calm and loving demeanor, he had raging anxiety and depression.

---

5. You're probably getting sick of Broken Record #1, but God isn't!
6. Ephesians 4:30; Mosiah 2:36; Mormon 1:14

President Smith was only 33 years old when he was called into the Quorum of the Twelve Apostles in 1903. His father John Henry Smith, who was also in the Quorum at that time, said of George, "He's not healthy. He won't last long." George suffered from chronic intestinal problems and frequent infections that were likely connected to his anxiety. He had periods where he needed to stay in bed for days at a time, largely in response to stressful situations or pushing his body too hard. He also confessed to having "delicate nerves" his whole life: "Even when things are normal, my nerves are not very strong." He had a strong desire to please everyone and follow the Lord exactly. Such a desire is very pure and wonderful unless it is overdone and overtakes your life and health.

George traveled extensively as an Apostle. On average, he traveled 30,000 miles per year, which is *a lot* when you don't have airplanes by which to travel.[7] Whenever he was on a church assignment, he felt guilty that he was neglecting his wife and three children. Whenever he was home fulfilling his family duties, he felt guilty that he wasn't out doing his work for the church. He could not find a balance among his duties that felt right to him; most of us with similar natures rarely do.

In 1909, he became quite ill.[8] He was fatigued, suffered from "a weak heart," had full body pains, and had a constant "nervous frustration." It was initially thought to be from the flu, though we don't know that for sure. Over the next three years, he could complete none of his church duties because of his symptoms. For a time, he lived in California, thinking the sea air would help. He also stayed in St. George for a time

---

7. Well, even if you do travel by plane, it's still a lot.
8. The details from these events come from a 2008 article: "Cheat the Asylum of a Victim": George Albert Smith's 1909–1912 Breakdown, by Mary Jane Woodger. It is extensively researched and very informative.

for a lower altitude when he didn't want to go back to California. He stayed in Arizona for the dry desert air. Elder Smith lived in a tent for months, trusting that the constant fresh air would help him. He also prayed and fasted regularly to be healthy. He received multiple blessings of healing. But none of it seemed to help. Most of us in a similar circumstance would wonder if our faith just wasn't enough.

This was all worsened because he assumed he was letting God and the church down. He wasn't able to even go to church, let alone attend to any of his responsibilities with being in the Quorum of the Twelve Apostles. His friends and family were supportive of him during this time, many of them providing similar advice to that given by King Benjamin in the Book of Mormon: "It is not requisite that a man should run faster than he has strength."[9] His uncle advised him to "dump your responsibility for a while before the hearse dumps your bones."

Sometime between 1909 and 1911, Elder Smith asked God to take his life; he and his wife Lucy began praying for his release from mortality.[10] He was worn out, both physically and spiritually. He feared the work of the Lord on the earth was being held back as a result of his illness. Elder Smith laid his life completely into the hands of the Lord. It's not quite the same as having suicidal intent, but what we may call passive suicidal ideation—he'd be better off dead (in his own mind) but he wasn't willing to take his own life.

And that's when things began to change. It didn't happen all at once, nor did it even happen quickly. But over roughly the next year, George began to recover slowly until he fully regained his abilities in 1912. The Lord did not take his life.

---

9. Mosiah 4:27

10. Lucy W. Smith as related to Bishop K. J. Fetzer and contained in a letter from Bishop Fetzer to the Smith children, August 7, 1953, *Smith Papers*, box 151, fd. 3. As cited in the article from Mary Jane Woodger.

So, what happened? Why did George begin to improve at that point? This is my theory—completely giving himself up to the Lord changed the way he approached his illness and life. It changed his thinking, and thus literally changed his brain. This seemed to have the same effect as cognitive-behavioral therapy (CBT), the most common therapy for anxiety and depression listed in chapter one. The goal of this type of therapy is to change your mindset and behavior to replace negative or destructive thoughts with positive ones to better guide your feelings and behavior. It helps you to better understand what drives your coping behaviors and reactions, and thus develop better skills for handling distressing thoughts or events. That's essentially what happened to Elder Smith. Did he have another medical illness that led to his emotional exhaustion? And if so, was it a resolution of this other illness that led to the improvement in his physical and mental functioning? We're not sure. Regardless, he had multiple signs of anxiety and depression, even if it was secondary to another health problem.

He continued to have bouts of depression and anxiety that affected his life until he died in 1951. But he could still be an elect servant of the Lord, serving as the eighth president of The Church of Jesus Christ of Latter-day Saints. He didn't have the benefit of medication or other tools like we do today, but he used everything that was at his disposal to get better.

He's not the only church leader to experience such things. President Gordon B. Hinckley said in his biography, "I have a sense of sadness and depression the last few days. It has almost overwhelmed me[. . .]. I have put on a veneer of smiles, but feel under a deep cloud of depression." Elder Jeffrey R. Holland, in the conference talk "Like a Broken Vessel" that is mentioned multiple times in this book, described depression as that "dark night of the mind and spirit." He even admitted, "I once terrifyingly saw it in myself."

The Book of Mormon prophet Alma experienced immense depression after the people in Ammonihah rejected his preaching. It took an angel to get him back to himself.[11] The sons of Mosiah experienced depression and were going to give up their missionary efforts among the Lamanites until they received comfort from the Spirit: "Now when our hearts were depressed, and we were about to turn back, behold, the Lord comforted us, and said[. . .]bear with patience thine afflictions, and I will give unto you success."[12] Not everyone gets this same promise in the immediate future, but we all get this promise to be fulfilled eventually. Joseph Smith cried out to the Lord when he was in the cold, wet, and dirty Liberty Jail, while he and all the Saints suffered: "O God, where art thou? And where is the pavilion that covereth thy hiding place? How long shall thy hand be stayed, and thine eye, yea thy pure eye, behold from the eternal heavens the wrongs of thy people and of thy servants, and thine ear be penetrated with their cries?" Joseph was beyond depressed and anxious and fearful and tired and frustrated by the difficulties he and his people experienced. The Savior, kind and wise as ever, responded by saying, "My son, peace be unto thy soul; thine adversity and thine afflictions shall be but a small moment; and then, if thou endure it well, God shall exalt thee on high."[13] God sees everything, even when we don't. I promise you that angels are with you supporting you, whether or not you see them.[14] God always wins, He always loves you, and you are in the same company as the prophets of old and modern times.

Two experiences place the problem of anxiety and depression in an even greater light. In the time leading up to Jesus's

---

11. Alma 8:9–14
12. Alma 26:27
13. Doctrine and Covenants 121:1–8
14. Doctrine and Covenants 84:88; 2 Kings 6:16

suffering in Gethsemane and on the cross, He showed some signs of significant depression. He frequently would pray all night for comfort. Jesus sought more assurance and closer friendship with His disciples. He even called for heavenly beings to come visit Him on the Mount of Transfiguration. The prophets Moses and Elijah appeared with Jesus before His disciples Peter, James, and John. Elder James E. Talmage in his incredibly important book *Jesus the Christ*, referring to what happened on the Mount of Transfiguration, said, "Unto Christ the manifestation was strengthening and encouraging. The prospect of the experiences immediately ahead must naturally have been *depressing and disheartening in the extreme*. In faithfully treading the path of His life's work, He had reached the verge of the valley of the shadow of death; and the human part of His nature called for refreshing" (emphasis mine).

At another time, during His pre-mortal existence, Enoch saw something that he almost couldn't imagine—Jehovah (or Jesus Christ) was weeping: "And Enoch said unto the Lord: How is it that thou canst weep, seeing thou are holy, and from all eternity to all eternity?. . . and naught but peace, justice, and truth is the habitation of thy throne; and mercy shall go before thy face and have no end; how is it thou canst weep?"[15] The answer is long, but in short, it is because the Savior is so sad and angry over the wickedness of the people on the earth that He almost can't take it. In order to have the utmost of joy throughout eternity, we also must know the full depths of sorrow. Jesus struggled too, but He did it all for us. We can overcome *with* Him and *because* of Him.

I relate to a lot of President Smith's story. I have had similar feelings of guilt, inadequacy, failure, and the sense that I am letting other people down. When on my mission, I would also

---

15. Moses 7:28–38

have to stay in bed with a non-specific illness for a few days every couple of months. My emotional state was too much for my body to bear, so I had to regain my strength periodically. Such times were filled with immense guilt and sadness. It's the same now when I have bouts of depression or severe anxiety. It doesn't happen anywhere near as often as it used to, but it does still happen. And you know what, God still loves me, just like He still loved George Albert Smith. He still loves you too,[16] even if you suffer. We shouldn't expect to overcome the trials of life by ourselves, because we can't. The Savior Jesus Christ gives us hope that we can overcome through Him. We need his grace to help us through. The ultimate goal of eternity is to become as He and our Heavenly Parents are, and it is impossible to do that on our own. Even when you are struggling to feel the Spirit, keep seeking Jesus![17] You may not see immediate results, but He is there more than you realize.

President Smith lived a full life and added immensely to the growth of God's kingdom on earth, despite his desire to achieve perfection in mortality and the mental health struggles this produced. I believe you and I can do the same.

COMMON CONCERN

▶ I feel so guilty because I have so much but I still feel really depressed all of the time. I love God but He must hate me for not appreciating what I have.

◁ Gratitude is a wonderful thing so that we can show God our appreciation of His gifts. But your brain simply works differently when you are in the middle of a mental illness. God knows this. He understands perfectly what we are going through and the

---

16. Broken Record #1! You get the idea.
17. Ether 12:41 (my favorite scripture)

limitations that places on our functioning. We are commanded to do the best we can within our circumstances, not to be without fault in this world. God does not hate you, but loves you more than you can imagine.[18]

---

18. Hmm, I wonder where you've read this before?

CHAPTER THREE

Anxiety Disorders

Nathan[1] is fourteen. Despite struggling with anxiety for many years, he still enjoys playing video games and being outside. In particular, he has a flight simulator game which helps him escape his concerns when he needs to. Sometimes he is overwhelmed by school assignments or other big things expected of him. He thinks about all the potential bad outcomes if he fails to do the assignment, and this overwhelms him even further. It becomes so debilitating sometimes that he lies to his parents to avoid negative consequences. "I get anxious when I lie about something. And that's why I lie usually, so I don't get in trouble because I didn't do something I was supposed to do." He often picks at his eyelashes or bites his fingernails when he is anxious. Sometimes his parents get upset with him when he exhibits these nervous habits.

---

1. Not his real name.

He has been on medication before, but it wasn't a good fit for him. "I was on a medication that was affecting the way I act. I said some things that I probably shouldn't have to friends, and they didn't want to be around me anymore, so they weren't my friends anymore. That was a really low point in my life. That's when I tried to cut myself." The deterioration of Nathan's friendships led him to cut his wrists. Thankfully, he didn't cut very deep, as he quickly realized that he didn't want to be truly dead or harm himself. He was lucky that he quickly had this realization before he caused himself any serious damage.

He was only on the medication for a short time, but the adjustment period to having a new substance in your body can be difficult. Sometimes things actually get worse before they get better. This is why it is so important to be open with your doctor, your family, and others you trust.

Nathan has met with a therapist regularly for quite a while. He thinks talking with someone about his anxiety has helped more than anything. "It's just important to talk about your feelings. I found that to be the most helpful."

◁▽ ◁▽ ◁▽

Katie[2] is only thirteen years old but has already experienced some extreme anxiety. Her family has often seen it cover up her sweet and caring spirit. As a young child, she had surgery on her hip and ended up wearing a cast for almost a year. She couldn't walk with her cast, so she had to spend nearly all her time with her mom who had to carry her around. After that experience, she showed a lot of separation anxiety—she really struggled when she had to be separated from her mother for any reason. She often has a hard time falling asleep on her

---

2. Not her real name.

own and wants her mom to lay by her; she then really struggles to sleep if her mom is not available. She can have a meltdown over what appears to be a small thing to others.

This has added stress to her mother, as Katie has difficulty building trust with others. "Sometimes I can't be her person," her mother Jennifer said. Jennifer[3] has included Katie's father and their other children in supporting her. "When you have anxiety, it definitely affects the whole family," Jennifer shared. The conversation with the rest of the family has been "she's hurting, and we need to deal with this together. We need to be patient with her *and try to separate what is her and what is her anxiety.*" Jennifer only recognized this as a significant issue in the last year or two, but Katie is improving as she and her family adapt to properly addressing her needs.

Would she have such severe anxiety if she hadn't needed the cast as a toddler? Or would it have happened regardless? There is no way to know. The stress of dealing with the COVID-19 pandemic seemed to have brought things to a head for her (like so many of us). She loves to socialize with her friends, but this obviously limited her, given the need to physically distance herself from others. Anxiety can be like an underwater river—it's always flowing, even though you can't see it. People with anxiety often have less emotional reserves to adapt to tough circumstances; it doesn't take much extra water to cause the river to flood.

⊿⊽ ⊿⊽ ⊿⊽

As you probably guessed, Nathan and Katie both have an anxiety disorder. To say that someone has an anxiety disorder is quite a non-specific term. Many people worry about things a lot but having a "worrying" personality is not the same as hav-

---

3. Not her real name, either.

ing an anxiety disorder. Remember Broken Record #3: anxiety (and depression) is a normal *emotion*, and it is appropriate to worry about certain things from time-to-time. But your anxiety can turn against you,[4] and in multiple different ways.

There are multiple different anxiety disorders. I have generalized anxiety disorder, probably the most common, but also some social anxiety. Other official DSM diagnoses from the latest edition include separation anxiety (difficulty separating yourself from a certain person, usually a parent), a specific phobia (more than just "I don't like spiders" but a severe anxiety response), a panic disorder (frequent panic attacks)[5], selective mutism (refusal to speak in certain situations, such as school), PTSD (reliving a horrific event or events from the past that caused you a lot of emotional or physical trauma),[6] or social anxiety (severe anxiety in social situations). You can also develop anxiety from certain medications, substances like drugs or alcohol, or from a different medical condition.

There is often a lot of confusion over the difference between anxiety and fear. The DSM says that *fear* is an "emotional response to real or perceived imminent threat," whereas *anxiety* is "anticipation of a future threat." Fear comes from something right in front of you; anxiety comes from something inside. For example, anxiety might be a big worry that your parents will get a divorce after you just heard them fighting, but fear is when the divorce actually happens, and it completely changes your life. There is some overlap of the two in this example, which can often happen.

---

4. Remember the robot butler?!

5. A panic attack is more than just a few moments of intense anxiety. Your heart races, your vision blurs, it's hard to breathe, you become lightheaded, and you feel as though you are dying. They can be very serious and are often mistaken for a heart attack.

6. PTSD is not classified as an Anxiety Disorder in the DSM, but I include it here as it can be similar to other anxiety disorders.

That doesn't mean anxiety isn't real, or that it's something we intentionally make up, or even that the upcoming event isn't something to worry about. Many of us often deal with this by avoiding these situations. For example, you may call in sick to school on the day when you have a big presentation, or you don't go to the school dance because you don't know anybody. Avoiding the situation doesn't really take away the guilt or nervousness.

Given that there are multiple different anxiety disorders, I won't include all the DSM-5 criteria.[7] There are many other screening tools to help along the way. One common tool is the Generalized Anxiety Disorder scale (GAD-7). It asks the following questions:

Over the last two weeks, how often have you been bothered by any of the following problems?

▷ Feeling nervous, anxious, or on edge?
▷ Not being able to stop or control worrying?
▷ Worrying too much about different things?
▷ Trouble relaxing?
▷ Being so restless that it is hard to sit still?
▷ Becoming easily annoyed or irritable?
▷ Feeling dread, as if something awful might happen?

You answer each question with not at all, several days, more than half the days, or nearly every day. There is a scoring system that can tell you whether the symptoms are mild, moderate, or severe. You get a sense by the types of questions asked, and potential answers given, how the severity of each person's experience guides whether it relates to a mental illness or normal emotions. Again, the GAD-7 and other simi-

---

7. It can also get very technical, boring, and sometimes confusing, even for professionals.

lar questionnaires are not a tool to diagnose anxiety but are screening tools to direct you on whether to pursue a more formal evaluation.

There are other symptoms that can go along with anxiety. Intrusive thoughts, such as negative or scary ideas that are difficult to get rid of, are common. Even just a constant, vague sense of being uncomfortable in your body can be a sign. Probably the biggest underlying theme to anxiety is a nervous anticipation that some future event will turn out terribly. And the anticipation can almost be worse than what actually happens. That's what makes life harder when you have clinical anxiety—your mind has made things worse than reality ever could.

While God may not *cure* **your illness, He can still** *heal* **you.** I continue to deal with significant anxiety and depression, and sometimes it weighs me down. However, I can work through it given what I have learned: continuing to go to therapy, continuing to use medication when I've needed it, and doing many of the little things that help.[8] I continue to cling to the covenants which I have made with God. I am not perfect at keeping the commandments, but that's okay. A righteous person is someone who is repenting, not someone who is perfect. He continues to heal me in ways to help me progress, and often it is our trials which do that. The Church's mental health website[9] points out that healing comes in stages, not all at once. Do your best, and He will do the rest. Why? Because (say it with me now) *He loves you!*

---

8. Such as what we listed in chapter one.
9. mentalhealth.churchofjesuschrist.org

CHAPTER FOUR

Depressive Disorders

I have known Emma[1] and her family for many years. She is very talented, and someone I've always enjoyed talking with. She is a wonderful friend and example to others, and I am always impressed with her attitude toward life and the way she reaches out to make others feel comfortable. Emma has a brilliant smile, but I didn't understand until many years of knowing her how much she buried behind that smile.

Emma had periods of "crashing" when she was in junior high. She would be completely fine, and then, without warning, become very depressed. She would experience a significant amount of guilt and get overwhelmed to the point where she was "not sure how to get back on track." She would miss school for days at a time, just staying in bed. Her grades suf-

---

1. You're probably noticing that I'm not using the real name of any of the teenagers in the book. That's because you are observant. Good job.

fered. Her relationship with friends suffered. She didn't think anyone would want to be her friend or get close to her. Even if they did, she wasn't sure she wanted them to know what was happening to her. Yet, she also felt she was being fake pretending everything was fine. "I hid it so well," she said. "No one saw what was really going on." She didn't like who she was and how she acted around others.

She wasn't sure what was happening to her. Emma had seen what depression looked like—her older sister and father both had it, but theirs was a lot worse. She would periodically come out of the darkness and feel like her old self, but her dad and sister had a tougher time getting to their baseline functioning. Compared to them, she hardly struggled at all. There was no way she was struggling from depression, she thought.

Despite not accepting that she had clinical depression, she agreed to see a therapist. This was eye-opening to her. "It helped lift me out of that rut that I was in," she said. She also credits the therapy with helping her relationships with family members. Given that some family members dealt with depression, it was easier to talk about once her therapist empowered her. Emma experienced no stigma, no embarrassment, and no shame from anyone in her family.

After a few months, her therapist left to work elsewhere. The following winter did not go well. Things worsened again, but this time she couldn't pull herself out of the "rut," even with the skills her therapist taught her and the coping skills she had developed. She appropriately went to see her doctor who diagnosed her with Major Depressive Disorder, the clinical name given to general clinical depression. She started medication, and "it has seriously changed everything. I still have hard days, but the medication has helped me immensely." She copes with her mood and symptoms so much better. She plays the piano every day to calm herself, not because she "has to" practice or because someone else wants her to; she just does it for herself. She writes in her journal often. She reads past entries to remember many of the lessons that she has learned from her experiences with depression.

Another important coping mechanism for her is a form of meditation. She prays, she reads her scriptures, and then just sits, listening to her own thoughts with no agenda at all. She relishes these opportunities. "It's helped me so much." But these efforts to communicate with God are somewhat new for Emma. When her depression first appeared in junior high, she had no testimony of the gospel and had no desire to gain one. "I just went to church because that's what you did. I didn't care. I didn't have a relationship with God, and I didn't care to. That was part of the depression."

Once she got to high school, she decided that maybe she did want the gospel to be a significant part of her life. But when a depressive episode would again hit, she began to doubt. "I would have lots of doubts, lots of questions. I would often second-guess myself. Do I really believe this? Am I really feeling the Spirit?" She had a hard time identifying the Spirit when depressed, and she wasn't sure it was worth moving forward with developing her testimony.

Types of depression

As we saw with anxiety, there are different forms of depression. Sometimes it's a specific diagnosis, and sometimes it's a combination of a couple of them. Keep in mind that it's not just that you have more sadness than at other times, it's the addition of other symptoms and how they affect your ability to live your life that makes it a medical concern.

One useful acronym doctors often use to remember the different symptoms of depression is **SIG E CAPS:**[2]

Sleep (either more or less but often more)

Interest (lack of interest in things you typically enjoy, also called *anhedonia*). The I can also stand for isolation, as it is common to isolate from other people.

Guilt (experiencing guilt over pretty much anything, but usually goes along with feelings of worthlessness)

Energy (lack of)

Concentration (difficulty with)

Appetite (usually less, sometimes increased)

Psychomotor (basically you just move differently, often like you are in slow motion)

Suicidal thoughts

As you could guess, the more of these symptoms you are showing, the more likely you are to have a major depressive disorder (i.e., clinical depression). There are other screening tools often used. The Patient Health Questionnaire 9 (PHQ-9) is a common tool. There are nine questions about the above symptoms where the patient estimates how often they have been experiencing these symptoms over the last two weeks (None, Several Days, More than Half the Days, Nearly Every Day). This then provides a score to help guide the severity of symptoms. It is especially helpful to have the questionnaire done repeatedly to see how you respond to treatment. Both tools help support a diagnosis, but the criteria in the DSM are the gold standard.

---

2. This is not an official way to diagnose depression but is a handy guide on what traits or symptoms to focus on. You should also note that doctors come up with weird acronyms, because that's just how we are.

When people think of "depression," they mostly are picturing Major Depressive Disorder (MDD). This is episodic, meaning you have a distinct period when there is a depressive episode and then you come out of it. Further episodes can occur, or it can just be one. For most people, there are multiple episodes. This is traditionally where people can't get out of bed, cry all the time, feel worthless, and any other severe form of the above-listed symptoms. To meet the diagnostic criteria, the episode must last for at least two weeks (though it often lasts longer), with a significant reduction of symptoms in-between episodes. If it is from grief over a tragic event, medication, drugs, or other medical problems, then it is not considered MDD.

The form of depression that seems to be constant but may allow you to still be reasonably functional in life is called Persistent Depressive Disorder, or dysthymia. This is where you experience the classic symptoms of depression, but not to the extreme that you would with MDD. It lasts for at least one year in children or adolescents, and at least two years in adults, to make the diagnosis. In some ways, this can be harder than MDD, as you never quite escape from the depression.

Dysthymia is probably much more common than MDD, but it's also not as noticeable. Sometimes you may think the person is grumpy or that it's just a part of their personality. Sometimes you may not see it in others at all. A lot of people, like Emma, are very good at hiding their emotions and struggles. Finding out I have anxiety and depression really surprised most of the people I know. While I've had at least one episode of MDD, Persistent Depressive Disorder probably fits my case a little better. I still feel depression occasionally, but since I have taken better care of myself and found some helpful medications, I don't feel it as often.

As I mentioned before, depression and anxiety are closely linked. They are like two sides of the same coin, connected closely but still slightly different. It is very common for an individual to have both depression and anxiety. I initially struggled only with anxiety when I was diagnosed in 2003. I developed depression in about 2009 once I started my residency training in Family Medicine. Since then, I have dealt with both and remain on medication. While it's hard, I'm not any less of a person because of it, and God loves me just as much as He did before. It's the same with you.

△▽ △▽ △▽

Sometimes the pendulum of depression swings to the other side. You may feel full of energy, so much so that you only need to sleep a few hours each night. You might have great new ideas or feel as though you can do anything. This often goes along with overestimating your own importance.[3] You can't keep your thoughts straight, and you're constantly distracted. You don't think very logically, sometimes doing things like going on big shopping sprees where you spend thousands of dollars you probably don't have. You may even start seeing or hearing things that aren't there.

This other extreme is called mania. When you've had an episode of mania, either with or without an episode of depression, you meet criteria for Bipolar Disorder.[4] Many people with bipolar have only ever experienced one episode of mania; recurring episodes of depression are much more common.

---

3. Sometimes this is hard to understand. You *are* very important because you are a child of God, but that doesn't mean that you are better than everyone else. That is what I mean by this. It is often called "delusions of grandeur."
4. "Bipolar" meaning "two poles," like the North and South Poles on the globe, completely opposite each other. Get it? Bipolar? Pretty clever, eh? Sorry, I guess doctors are impressed with stupid things sometimes.

The episodes can occur years apart so that people with bipolar don't even know they have it until they're adults. Bipolar doesn't happen often in teenagers, but when it does, it is so disruptive that it can completely derail their whole life. Many don't recognize that they are in a manic state, and even if they do, they like it because they are more creative and get more done. But they also make very poor decisions that can harm their bodies and spirits.

You may remember from the Introduction that bipolar can be either, or both, a thought disorder and a mood disorder. Some people become psychotic when in the middle of a manic episode. Psychosis is when your thoughts and emotions are impaired so much that you lose touch with reality. You may have auditory (hearing) or visual (seeing) hallucinations. Some may become suspicious of others or have multiple delusions (false beliefs).

The combination of these effects on your thoughts and mood makes it harder to feel the Spirit than with most other forms of mental illness. Though we have heard from everyone interviewed in this book that mental illness makes it harder to feel the Spirit and God's love for us, we don't know how this works. There are certain ways in which our spirit body interacts with our physical body, as well as with the Holy Spirit, that we just don't understand. How our physical bodies feel the Spirit of God, with sensations like peace, happiness, love, comfort, and others[5] is not something we learn in this life. But mental illness seems to disrupt this. Essentially, mental illness is a malfunction of your brain's ability to communicate with itself, and this then leads to a disruption in the way our spirit and physical body communicate. We then can't communicate with the Holy Spirit very easily.

---

5. Galatians 5:22–23

Does this mean it is impossible to recognize the Spirit's impact when we are in the throes of mental illness? Does it mean having a mental illness takes away our agency? Do we lack enough control over our thoughts and moods to be held fully accountable for our actions? We don't have a full understanding of how this works, but I believe that the answer to these questions is a qualified 'No'. We know God understands the unique circumstances each of us faces, and so there is probably not an answer that is generalizable to every person. Jesus is the judge of all humanity, so part of having faith in Him is trusting that His judgements are just, but also merciful. It can be a dissatisfying answer to hear that we don't know and simply must trust that our Savior Jesus Christ knows what He is doing, but I actually find comfort in the fact that I don't have to be the one to figure out how each person's experience fits into these tough conditions. This applies to all mental illnesses, not just bipolar that we've been talking about in these last few paragraphs.

Joseph Smith said, "The great Jehovah contemplated the whole of the events connected with the earth, pertaining to the plan of salvation, before it rolled into existence[. . .]. He knows the situation of both the living and the dead, and has made ample provision for their redemption, *according to their several circumstances*, and the laws of the kingdom of God" (italics added).[6]

Remember (here we go again)—***God always loves you!*** And He gets you and will support you now and in the future in the way you need.

◿▽ ◿▽ ◿▽

---

6. From *Teachings of the Prophet Joseph Smith.*

Emma's connection with the Lord occurred at the same time she began taking medication in the middle of her junior year of high school. "I just felt so much better," she said. "I really began to work on my testimony by praying and reading the scriptures. It was a long process to come to God, but I feel Him now in my life." At the time of our interview, she was on her school's seminary council, and is looking forward to serving a mission.

It took Emma a while to recognize that depression does not look the same in every person. While many of the signs among different people are similar, she does not experience it the same way as her sister and dad, who have been hit very hard with it for a much longer time. "It's so different for [my sister compared to me]. Accepting that was a big bridge I had to cross." Because of this, she can't always tell who is suffering or not, so she has become a great advocate for others by sharing her own experiences. Her openness has helped a lot of other kids work through their own struggles.

Emma still has a wonderful smile and now it more sincerely reflects how she feels inside.

Anti-Depression and Anti-Anxiety Medications

Doctors and scientists talk about different classes of medications. A medication in each class has a similar effect on your body as any other in the same class. There are multiple classes of medications to treat depression and anxiety, and multiple drugs within each class. Some classes and some specific medications work better than others, both overall and for certain individuals. For example, if a medication worked well for a family member with the same diagnosis, it is more likely to work well for you. Many times, the first medication tried doesn't work well, and so it takes some trial and error to find a medication that gives you the maximum desired effect. In certain cases, more than one medication is needed, usually from different classes, to make an illness manageable. Medications also work best when taken together with therapy. It's uncommon for a doctor to give you medication without recommending therapy as well.

Doctors take a few things into account when considering what medication may be the best for the patient:

1. **Diagnosis**   Obviously, the condition that you are trying to treat drives a lot of the treatment. What type of depression or anxiety is it? For example, a medication called paroxetine is more effective for people who suffer from PTSD but is not used as often as some others for generalized anxiety disorder.

2. **Genetics**   Mental illness runs in families. If you have a family member with any sort of mental illness, it doesn't guarantee that you do too but puts you at a higher risk. Not only this, but how well a medication can work for you is also genetic. If you have depression like your mother and a certain medicine worked for her, it is more likely to work for you too. Different enzymes process different medications in our body. How well those specific enzymes work (or how much is present) in our own body is different from person to person and can affect how the medicine works.

3. **Side Effects**   Every medication has side effects, no matter how well it works. Most of the best medicines for different mental illnesses have similar side effects, though one may be worse than another or may just affect you differently than it would someone else. For example, the first medication I tried was fluoxetine (Prozac). It worked very well for my anxiety but gave me a lot of nausea. Other people don't experience that on fluoxetine, and I've since tolerated some other medicines a lot better.

4. **Cost** Medications can be very expensive. There are always new and promising drugs available to treat any number of diseases. But most of them for different mental illnesses offer little beyond what we already have. Using an older medication (which tends to have more reasonable prices) is often just as good as the new, expensive one. And for many of us, our insurance or income just can't cover the higher price.

All of these factors are important to consider. It is also important to note that medications receive regulatory approval for only certain conditions, so it's often unwise to prescribe a specific medicine for your condition if it's not approved to treat that. Sometimes it's appropriate, but not often. This is even more important when selecting a medication approved for youth. You and your doctor should work together to find out what best fits your needs.

Medications for depression and anxiety often take as long as six-to-eight weeks to reach their full benefit. Some teenagers may have an increase in suicidal thoughts when starting medications, but the pros of taking medication far outweigh the risks for those with a significant disease.

Medication Class[1]	Medication[2]	Anxiety	Depression	Common Side Effects[3]
Selective Serotonin Reuptake Inhibitors (SSRIs)	Fluoxetine (Prozac)	X	X	Headache, stomach upset, sleep changes, sexual issues, agitation
	Citalopram (Celexa)	X	X	
	Escitalopram (Lexapro)	X	X	
	Sertraline (Zoloft)	X	X	
	Fluvoxamine (Fluvox)	X	X	
	Paroxetine (Paxil)	X	X	
Selective norepinephrine-reuptake inhibitors (SNRIs)[4]	Venlafaxine (Effexor)	X	X	Nausea, dry mouth, sleep changes, constipation, sexual issues
	Desvenlafaxine (Pristiq)		X	
	Bupropion (Wellbutrin)		X	
	Duloxetine (Cymbalta)	X	X	
Tricyclic antidepressants[5]	Imipramine (Tofranil)		X	Dry mouth, constipation, Heart rhythm problems

---

1. Much of this information comes from the website www.uptodate.com.

2. The classes and medications listed are only those studied and found appropriate for use in adolescents or children. Some have been found to be more effective than others.

3. Not everyone experiences these side effects, and the vast majority of those who do get over them in a couple of weeks, so *do not be scared away* if you need the medication.

4. Most of these have not been extensively studied in adolescents, aside from venlafaxine.

5. Rarely used

Medication Class[1]	Medication[2]	Anxiety	Depression	Common Side Effects[3]
Benzodiazepines	Clonazepam	✗		Drowsiness, irritability, addiction potential
Stimulants	Guanfacine	✗		Abdominal upset, drowsiness, dizziness, irritability

COMMON QUESTION

▶ **I don't want to take medicine because my friend told me that it will change my personality and make me feel numb. Is that what medication does to you?**

◁ All medications have side effects, but they do not change who you are. Often the opposite is true—they can restore your personality. If you have changed from who you used to be because of your mental struggles, medication can help bring you back to who you want to be by addressing the illness. Your doctor can help you figure out if any negative effects are from the medication or from something else.

CHAPTER FIVE

Obsessive Compulsive Disorder (OCD)

James[1] and I spoke together on a sunny spring day. He has an upbeat disposition, which only added to the beauty of the day. He is easy to talk to, and it was very apparent that he speaks with much wisdom and experience. I knew he had faced some specific challenges in his young life but had no idea how far they went when I first talked to him for this book.

James has struggled with anxiety since he was in kindergarten. He wouldn't speak in his class, or to any adults other than his parents for a long time.[2] It started around the time his parents got divorced. His anxiety worsened throughout his

---

1. Name has been changed.
2. See the chapter on anxiety. Remember when we mentioned 'Selective Mutism'? This is a perfect example.

teenage years, along with a blossoming depression. He eventually became suicidal because life wasn't what he thought it should be.

So why are we mentioning this in the OCD chapter? Well, James found out in his early twenties that OCD was underlying the anxiety he had experienced for so long. He had not considered this until his therapist pointed it out. Anxiety disorders and various types of OCD are closely related. While it doesn't explain all of his anxiety, James definitely sees it as part of his struggles. "I just need things to be perfect, and I need to be in control."

I couldn't explain OCD any better than that. A desire to control your circumstances (and often other people's circumstances and behavior) is quite common, even if you don't have a mental illness. However, at its core, OCD encompasses the need to keep everything just the way you think it should be. There are two key aspects to OCD: obsessions and compulsions (hence the name). *Obsessions* are repetitive intrusive thoughts, fears, or urges that are not wanted or invited. *Compulsions* are the repetitive behaviors we do in response to any obsessions.

For example, James likes everything to be in order. He *has* to put his shoes away when he takes them off. The extreme mess he perceives is an obsessive thought, so the compulsion is putting the shoes away. I'm sure all of you have had your mom or dad tell you to put your shoes away, but James's anxiety over having his shoes on the floor was excessive. He underwent some *exposure therapy*, a type of therapy that is common for people with OCD. The therapy exposes the individual to whatever event or circumstance causes their obsessions and compulsions. The idea is to help them realize they can overcome their thoughts and actions without causing any negative outcomes. James's therapist told him he had to leave his shoes in the middle of the living room all night, and he could not put them away until he woke up for the day. James did it, but he did not sleep all night because of his obsession with tidiness. The notion of leaving his shoes out seemed preposterous to him—why would anybody do that?!—but actually doing it completely ruined his night. He got up for the day at five AM just so he wouldn't have to wait any longer to put his shoes away. It was really hard for him, but being exposed to the obsessive thoughts without performing the compulsive behavior taught him that nothing bad happens if he left his shoes out. He engaged in many rounds of exposure therapy, and he now feels he is in a much better place. He still wants his shoes put away, but he doesn't lose sleep if they are not.[3]

A need for control in life is very common after experiencing significant trauma in childhood. James's parents got divorced when he was about five years old. Divorce is tough on everybody in the family, but this is an extremely difficult age to deal with such a significant change in your family. I'm sure many of you reading this have been through your parents' divorce. There are so many emotions, fears, and mental scars that go along with it. The challenge of getting used to a new step-dad or step-mom, and maybe step-siblings, is significant. There is nothing easy about it for anyone, but especially the kids.

Following the divorce, his mother had to deal with raising James and his siblings alone while trying to work. She drank alcohol heavily to help ease her stress and soon became an alcoholic. Turning to drugs and alcohol is a frequent response to stress and mental illness by many adolescents and adults. It can sometimes dull the emotional and mental pain in the

---

3. It is VERY important that you don't try to do exposure therapy on your own. It can be very dangerous to try this without the help of a therapist.

short-term but makes it much worse in the long-term. As soon as the alcohol or other drugs wear off, the same struggles come right back to you, which can then often lead to further use and development of an addiction. All this use causes us to further lose control of our own thoughts and behavior as we lose many brain functions that we normally have.[4] The children of, and others close to, those who use drugs or other substances regularly perceive a lack of control in their own life because of how the person using drugs influences them. James had to deal with his mother's erratic behavior when she was drinking. His mom never hit him or his siblings, but she grabbed his arm tightly enough to leave bruises on multiple occasions. He nevertheless felt he needed to protect his siblings from her, and so tried to keep them away when his mother was drunk or particularly upset. James ended up making most of the meals for himself and his siblings, helped them with their homework, and otherwise filled a parenting role from a young age.

To add to these negative experiences, his best friend's father died by suicide when James was about fourteen. Being so close to someone who died by suicide set James on a downward spiral. He began having panic attacks and felt less and less in control of his life. He would fall into a deep depression at times, going days or weeks without going to school. This did not go along with his expectation that he should have perfect grades, so this failure to engage fully in his schooling only added to his sense of loss of control and guilt. He didn't have many friends, and his avoiding school only exacerbated his social isolation.

---

4. For example, drinking alcohol significantly slows down your reaction time, which is why it is so dangerous to drink and drive. Please, please, *please* promise me you will never drink and drive! By you reading that last sentence, I consider myself promised. Good job.

His mom would get angry and confused when James stayed home from school. She didn't understand what was going on with him. He began seeing a therapist after his friend's dad died by suicide and was on medication for a time. His therapist discussed with him how many of his problems originated with his anger towards, and sense of betrayal by, his mother. But James hated confrontation and wouldn't talk with his mother about the underlying causes of his anxiety and OCD. This led to him shutting down emotionally. "I just got to the point where I felt really numb to things," he said, "and I think that was just my mind coping; I just stopped feeling altogether."

James went to church. He prayed and read his scriptures, went to seminary and his youth activities. He was doing what he was taught to do in his church meetings, but it wasn't working. Wasn't the gospel about happiness? He described it like this: "I saw my peers and how they were acting, and I perceived them as being really happy and excited all the time, but I didn't feel like that. I thought I was supposed to feel that way." He expected the Spirit to be in his life, but he didn't notice it. He now felt abandoned not only by his father in the divorce and his mother in her drinking, but also by his Father in Heaven. "I was convinced that if God cared about me, I wouldn't be feeling like that because I was doing all the things He was asking me to."

So many of us experience this with our emotional challenges. The scriptures and our church leaders have made it clear that we need to do these basic things to be close to the Spirit and to feel happiness. But as it was for James, certain things in life can keep us from feeling the Spirit. It doesn't mean the Spirit is gone, just that the illness in our physical body keeps us from communicating with it as well. The promise of the sacrament—that "[we] may always have His Spirit to be with [us]"—remains in force as we try to keep the commandments. The Lord loves you[5] and will *not* abandon you, though it is very understandable to believe the opposite when you are in the thick of such a trying experience as mental illness.

Obsessive thoughts and compulsive behaviors are the hallmark of OCD. The rules around a person's compulsions are very rigid, so they must be done perfectly. If not, the individual struggles to calm their anxiety and often repeat it until they get it "right." It can include just touching certain things in a specific order, doing a certain movement before going through a door, or repeating certain words in your head. This sometimes keeps people from certain activities or otherwise disrupts their life. It's highly distressing if they do not perform the ritual correctly. Some people recognize their compulsions are not normal or do not have any connection to the obsessive thoughts, but many don't.

There are a few different types of OCD per the DSM-5, including the following:

1. **OCD**—basically the classic symptoms we usually think of, consistent with James's story. Other symptoms that can go along with the obsessions and compulsions can include the following:
    ▷   Excessive cleanliness, such as having to wash your hands multiple times in a row to ensure they are *really* clean.
    ▷   Excessive tidiness, much like James's severe anxiety about things not being put away in their own place.
    ▷   Depression. James couldn't get out of bed for days and weeks and missed school because of a deep depression.

---

5. Don't forget Broken Record #1!

▷ Preoccupation with safety, such as repeatedly checking that the door is locked, or the stove is off.

▷ Rituals. These are certain compulsions that one feels the need to perform before a given event, such as a particular routine that needs to be completed before bed or leaving the house.

▷ Motor tics. These are basically rituals that involve body movements or sounds that one makes repeatedly, either to calm anxiety or remove disturbing thoughts. Sometimes they are intentional by the person, and sometimes the person doesn't even notice that they occur.

▷ Excessive hoarding of money or other things. This is an attempt to have control over materials and any potential future problem.

2. **Hoarding Disorder.**[6] Those with a hoarding disorder feel incredible distress at the thought of getting rid of certain (or all) items. This leads to abundant clutter that can affect the safety and cleanliness of their home.

3. **Trichotillomania** (pulling out your own hair) and **excoriation** (skin-picking) are also different OCD disorders. They are a good example of repetitive compulsions that lead a person to harm their own body. It can be mild, where few if any people can sense that it is occurring or can be so severe as to be life-threatening.

4. **Body Dysmorphic Disorder,** or perceived flaws in your body or appearance not observable by others, is another one. This differs from an eating disorder or general ideas about looking good. One example is that people become obsessed

---

6. People can still engage in some hoarding even with something else as their primary diagnosis. See how complicated these diagnoses can get?!

with their body's build, thinking they are deformed. This leads to lots of mental and physical repetitive compulsions that can include staring into a mirror for hours each day and avoiding social situations. Some turn to surgery or other procedures to "fix" the problem. Some go so far as to have a leg or arm amputated to fit their desired look.

There is a strong connection between individuals with OCD and suicide, often because individuals cannot get away from these upsetting thoughts and behaviors. Lots of people say in jest that "It's just my OCD kicking in," but the actual condition can be deeply serious.

Treatment

You're probably noticing a trend about treatments about the conditions we are talking about. The basic self-care behaviors, such as exercise and a healthy diet, are a *must*! When these things aren't enough, therapy and medication are required. Cognitive-Behavioral Therapy (CBT), which we've discussed before, is also highly effective in OCD. The exposure therapy that we mentioned above, officially called Exposure and Response Prevention (ERP), is a subset of CBT that can be difficult for a person to engage in but is extremely effective. Our natural response is to avoid something that scares us or makes us uncomfortable, but that only buries it inside for it to erupt later. ERP helps us to face those fears or obsessions, and thus conquer them, but it can be very harmful to try it without the guidance of a therapist.

The same medications used for anxiety and depression can also work for OCD. Only some of them have official regulatory approval for people with OCD (see the table in the Extra Credit section about medications).

James's biggest piece of advice is to talk with others and be open about your struggles.[7] However, he also admits that talking with someone was the last thing he wanted to do. Not only did James feel like he couldn't talk with his mom about their relationship, but he didn't think others would understand. "So many people think [mental illness] is fake, so I didn't want to talk about it with anyone. I felt like, 'you have no idea what I'm experiencing.'"

It is so easy to feel that we are stranded on a deserted island or that no one understands. Thankfully, others do not have to face your exact experiences to understand your feelings. Someone who sincerely wants to connect with you in your trials (such as a loving parent or friend) can be filled with empathy and go along with you on your journey. Understanding what someone is going through is more about being present and willing to listen. Also, there are literally millions of other people who have had similar feelings and thoughts. This may be a great time to look for a support group of people with similar experiences with whom you can share your burden.

James points out four benefits he sees to talking openly about your emotional and mental state:

1. **It validates your emotions.** This is an incredibly important aspect of discussing your thoughts and emotions. While it may change none of the underlying issues, just understanding that you are not alone and what you feel is real helps immensely in your journey.

2. **It helps you recognize you are not "crazy."** Crazy is a loaded word that has no positive use. You are not crazy, no matter what your diagnosis is or how difficult you find things.

---

7. You're probably noticing that this is common advice from all the people I interviewed. That's because it's good advice.

3. **It helps you recognize the absurdity of some of your thoughts or fears.**   A lot of the thoughts that enter our heads when we have OCD or any other mental illness really have no point. They are random, illogical, and simply make little sense a lot of the time. But they are still there and often hard to get rid of.

4. **It provides greater clarity for yourself and others about what you feel.**   Much like validating your emotions, talking with trusted individuals can help you make sense of what you are experiencing and how it affects your life. It is a great early step to understanding what will help you the most in the treatment process.

"How will there be progress if you're not talking about it?" This is such great wisdom from James.

James continues to go to therapy. He went on medication for a while. He even called the national suicide hotline[8] once when he felt terribly alone. In the end, he needed to leave home to find God again. Most of us don't have to do that, but James's situation was somewhat unique. He can feel the Spirit again and now recognizes many of the ways God was with him for all those years. But it took addressing his physical, emotional, and spiritual needs all together to get to this point. Fasting and prayer and scripture study weren't enough; he needed more of a boost than church could provide, and there is nothing wrong with that. God *still* loves you. Part of how He shows that love is by providing wonderful scientific understanding and breakthroughs that can help us come back to Him, no matter how bad the trials may be. Never forget Him because He never forgets you.

---

8. The number again is 988.

James is now working towards a career in healthcare, which makes me happy. He is well on his way to achieving his goals. He couldn't have done that without fully engaging in the treatment process.

CHAPTER SIX

Suicide

As Noah[1] was finishing his sophomore year in high school, his typical coping skills weren't helping as much as they once did. He had always enjoyed working on cars and listening to music, but they were no longer enough to help him through his depression and negative thoughts. He had talked about this with his friends before, and they had always been a big support for him, but his hatred towards himself grew to where he felt he was better off dead.

He had a plan of exactly how he would die. As he was preparing to do it, he had "an overwhelming feeling of 'You shouldn't do it. It's not worth it.'" This gave him enough pause that he thought more about the consequences of his actions. Instead of going through with it, he called his friend to talk.

---

1. Yep, you guessed it—not his real name.

She came and sat with him while her dad called the police. He was taken to the hospital and admitted for suicidal ideation (or suicidal thoughts and actions).

Noah had suffered from depression for years. He described it primarily as extremely negative self-talk. "I was saying things like, 'You're stupid. You're a burden on others. You should just kill yourself.'" He couldn't escape this view of himself. Everyone tells a certain story about themselves, and his was a completely negative one, like many of us have.

He had been on medication for about five years, but it didn't seem to work. He had met with therapists, but the one he connected with the most retired and Noah hadn't been able to find one he liked since. While he was in the hospital, the doctor changed his medication and he engaged in therapy for nearly two weeks. He didn't like being there because it separated him from his usual coping methods (cars, music, and friends), but overall it did help.

Even though Noah received treatment for depression for many years, many people who die by suicide may not have a diagnosed mental illness. Suicide is driven by a combination of a desire to get rid of pain and despair, and believing that death is the only way to end it. This is partly why it can be so difficult to predict suicide. Every person who either attempts or dies by suicide has a different way of getting to that point. Victoria Hatton, a high school psychologist, has worked with numerous students with suicidal thoughts and behaviors. She points out that around twenty percent of high school students in the United States seriously consider suicide every year, with about nine percent actually attempting to kill themselves.[2] "Even though about one in every five kids have

2. The numbers are roughly similar for middle school students, though the data isn't as robust.

thought about suicide in the last year, it's within the realm of normal," she says. "If you have that thought, it doesn't mean that you have mental illness, it doesn't mean that you're broken, and it doesn't mean that there's something wrong with you. It means that probably something hard is happening in your life and you want it to stop[. . .]. If the thought [of suicide] pops into your head and it scares you or doesn't go away, you need to go talk to somebody."

We often just don't know what to do with the emotional pain we feel. As a teenager, you are still developing emotionally and you may not be used to some of the feelings or thoughts you have. It might be the worst anxiety you have ever felt and you're not sure if it will ever go away. But that doesn't mean that you have a mental illness; it just means that you're normal.

Though it is nearly impossible to know how someone may react in certain stressful situations, there are risk factors we can watch for. Every person has both internal and external behaviors or responses to various stressors in their environment when they struggle. Internal behaviors are often difficult for others to see. For example, when I am anxious, I recite numbers or think up stories to calm me down. Others likely don't know I am doing this. But we can observe external behaviors. I sometimes develop tics when I am nervous, like squeezing my hands hard into fists or nodding my head a lot. These are signs that something is bothering me.

Even if your externalization of your stress isn't as obvious as mine, we all have them. Maybe we have certain facial expressions, exhibit irritability, or even lash out in a physically aggressive manner. We might stop going to school out of embarrassment or because of pressure we feel to succeed. Often we don't want to take part in activities that we usually enjoy.³ Those close to us often recognize certain patterns in our behavior and what it might mean. These are signs we can look for in loved ones, friends, or others that could be a cause for concern.

However, stress or anxiety or depression or any other mental illness doesn't always lead to suicide attempts. In fact, **many people who attempt or succeed in killing themselves do not have a diagnosable mental illness at all.** Suicide comes from despair, from feeling such intense emotional (or sometimes physical) pain that you want to end it, and death is seen as the only way to do that. A significant number of suicide attempts are only decided upon in the moment, meaning the person wasn't planning or expecting to do it. The pain may have come on so suddenly, or build to such an unmanageable intensity they can no longer stand, that they simply react by harming themselves. Only half of all suicidal thoughts last longer than ten minutes. Certainly the thoughts can return, but they often continue to be short-lived.

Others, like Noah, consider it for a while, develop a specific plan for how they will do it, and then create the opportunity. They often feel a disconnection from happiness, social isolation, or hopelessness. They may feel like they are a burden to others. Sometimes the desire to kill oneself is rooted in the false belief that our loved ones, or others around us, would be better off if we were gone. Remember President George Albert Smith from chapter two—he prayed that God would end his life because he thought his illness and inability to serve was holding back the growth and progression of the church. His church leaders and colleagues (and apparently, God too) dis-

---

3. This is anhedonia like we mentioned in the depression chapter, but it doesn't always go along with a clinical diagnosis of depression.

agreed with him. *It is not the case that others will be better off with us dead.*

It is very common for people to blame themselves for a loved one's suicide. It's typical for them to think, "What did I do wrong that caused this? What should I have done? How did I not see this coming?" Immense guilt, confusion, and anger are often experienced by those left behind. Comfort can be hard for them to find. The ripples of suicide are felt by hundreds, often thousands, of people.

Many experts actually think that we may be approaching people who have suicidal thoughts in the wrong way. The person who is having suicidal thoughts is experiencing some sort of emotional pain and death seems the only option to end that pain. When we try to stop them from killing themselves, we may be unintentionally telling that person that we want them to keep having their pain. It doesn't always make sense, and they can interpret it as cruel instead of helpful. We should instead approach it as helping the suicidal person to increase their resilience and access to joy, which helps them find relief from their pain. Ms. Hatton, the school psychologist mentioned above, relates this to a knee surgery. Physical therapy helps to support the knee by strengthening the surrounding muscles. It adds protection to the area of pain and injury through better support. The solution is to reduce or eliminate the pain by reinforcing the joint, not by eliminating the leg altogether. When someone is considering suicide, they need support from people they love and trust. They also need professional help to develop and use the skills to overcome their challenges, instead of ending their pain through suicide.

The most common way in which adolescents attempt suicide is by overdosing on medication. Think about what pills are in your home and about ways to limit access to large amounts. Some families keep all their medicine locked in a cabinet, or they are only available from a parent. It is also important to be safe with guns. Limiting access to guns through safely storing them, locking them up, or even removing them from the house if someone in your home is having suicidal thoughts, is wise and often necessary. Better protecting medication and guns may not be enough to prevent them from accessing these dangers or taking their own life, but it at least limits their options if they are considering suicide. Putting distance between the thought and dangerous items has shown to be effective in decreasing attempts.

Teenagers are also more likely to harm themselves without a full suicide attempt—approximately ten-to-twenty percent have done so. Cutting or burning on arms or legs are common ways to do this. Often the individual has an emotional "release" with this action, an almost calming effect, though the release may not last very long. Sometimes it is attention-seeking or a way by which a teen can communicate that they need help, but more often it is for another reason entirely. It may be a result of significant self-loathing, and thus a way to punish themselves. Some teenagers describe it as a way to stop feeling numb. It could be that this is a way a teenager tries to exert some sort of control over their life. Sometimes they just don't know how else to feel an emotional relief. Individuals who cut themselves are more likely to die by suicide, but the cutting behavior is rarely an attempt to die; more often it is an invitation to find other ways to address their emotions and thoughts.

⊿⊽ ⊿⊽ ⊿⊽

The question of the eternal consequence for those who die by suicide is very troubling to many people, and is so misunderstood, that it deserves a lot of attention. ***Those who die by suicide do not automatically go to hell, or the Telestial King-***

dom, or any other undesirable place for eternity. Did you get that? This is an extremely important point that *you need to understand*. If someone tells you that dying by suicide means you go to hell, they are mistaken. There are so many factors that go into our salvation that we cannot reduce our eternal progression to one act, nor are we the ultimate judge determining where someone ends up. We do not have all the information or context for each individual or see them in the same way that the Lord does. We are not in a position to pass fair judgement. Here are some thoughts of church leaders over the years on this topic:

> **Elder Bruce R. McConkie:** *"Persons subject to great stresses may lose control of themselves and become mentally clouded to the point that they are no longer accountable for their acts. Such are not to be condemned for taking their own lives. It should also be remembered that judgment is the Lord's;* he knows the thoughts, intents, and abilities of men; and he in his infinite wisdom will make all things right in due course" (emphasis mine).[4]

> **Elder M. Russell Ballard:** "I feel that the Lord . . . recognizes differences in intent and circumstances: Was the person who took his life mentally ill? Was he or she so deeply depressed as to be unbalanced or otherwise emotionally disturbed? Was the suicide a tragic, pitiful call for help that went unheeded too long or progressed faster than the victim intended? Did he or she somehow not understand the seriousness of the act? Was he or she suffering from a chemical imbalance that led to despair and a loss of self-control?
>
> "Obviously, we do not know the full circumstances surrounding every suicide. *Only the Lord*

---

4. As quoted in the LDSLiving.com article cited in the Bibliography.

knows all the details, and he it is who will judge our actions here on earth.

"When he does judge us, I feel he will take all things into consideration: our genetic and chemical makeup, our mental state, our intellectual capacity, the teachings we have received, the traditions of our fathers, our health, and so forth" (emphasis mine).[5]

Elder Dale G. Renlund: "I believe that in the vast majority of cases, we'll find that [those who have died by suicide] have lived heroic lives, and that that suicide will not be a defining characteristic of their eternities.[6]

"This doesn't mean killing oneself is acceptable in the eyes of the Lord. Elder Ballard has also said, "Suicide is a sin—a very grievous one, yet the Lord will not judge the person who commits that sin strictly by the act itself. The Lord will look at that person's circumstances and the degree of his accountability at the time of the act."

President Spencer W. Kimball added to that thought: "To commit suicide is a sin *if one is normal in his thinking*"[7] (emphasis mine).

Suicide is serious in both an immediate and eternal sense, but it does not equate to eternal damnation.

△▽ △▽ △▽

You're probably wondering, so what do I do if someone I care about is considering suicide? The good news is that you don't need to be an expert. You don't need an advanced degree, or even have experienced those feelings and thoughts yourself.

---

5. This is a fantastic article from the October 1987 issue of the *Ensign*.
6. Taken from his video testimony on churchofjesuschrist.org.
7. Also quoted in the LDSLiving.com article.

All you need to do is to reach out in love. Just be there. Maybe that sounds too simple, but it really is true much of the time. Often, we just need to know that there are others who care about us, no matter what we have done. Some people may be so ashamed of having these thoughts, or even having attempted suicide in the past, that they can't bear to face the world. They need a helping hand.

Besides just being there for them, you should also include professional help for the individual. All circumstances are different for resources in your area, but you can always call the police or take the person to the hospital if they are serious about their intention to die. There is a national emergency number (988) that you or they can call at any time some help is needed, or even just a listening ear. While your bishop is (usually) not a trained professional in mental health, he can help connect you with church and community resources. Sometimes people who are having suicidal thoughts just don't know where to turn or even have the motivation or courage to pick up the phone to start the treatment process. You can help with this.

Elder Renlund has reminded us, "We shouldn't underestimate the importance of the church as a community, coming together and helping each other through this life. Heavenly Father knew it would be a challenge, and He knew we would need each other's help."[8]

△▽ △▽ △▽

Noah is not unique in his pain, but he was blessed with the ability to know what to do about it. His thoughts were redirected when he was about to kill himself, and he reached out to a trusted friend. I believe it was the Spirit telling him not

---

8. Stated in the same video mentioned above.

to do it, and giving him a picture of what the consequences of suicide would be for him and those close to him. He was blessed that his friend was kind enough to sit with him for a while, and even that she was available to do so. He was blessed that he had the medical resources around him to be hospitalized. Yes, you heard that right—*he was blessed that he could be hospitalized.* It saved his life. He had the blessing of medication and doctors and therapists and a loving family. Not everyone is so lucky.

He fully recognizes those blessings. He admits he has grown closer to his friends, because they helped him. "A lot of it has helped me become a better friend," he said. "I see what they are willing to do for me. It has also helped me become more sympathetic and more willing to help people." He feels closer to his parents: "They helped me through the whole thing, and they didn't say, 'You don't need treatment.' They supported me through going to the hospital and getting medicine and therapists. They never made me feel ashamed or bad about it." But most importantly, he feels nearer to God: "He knows what's going on in my life, and He knows what type of people I need to be around, and he's provided those type of people to help me through it. It's helped me come closer to Him."

Noah offers some great final advice for other teenagers: "Depression sucks, but there is a lot of good that comes out of it; it's not all bad. It's also not all good, but it definitely helps you realize that a lot more people than you think suffer from mental illness, and a lot more people hide it. If you catch onto it, you can help them a lot, just by saying 'hi,' or checking up on them." Knowing he had someone to talk to is what saved his life. Even if you don't have a friend or family member you trust to talk to, everyone has somebody—everyone has God.

COMMON CONCERN

▶   **I worry that talking to my child or other kids about suicide makes them more likely to physically harm themselves.**

◁   The exact opposite is true. Talking in an open and honest manner about the seriousness of suicide with our children or friends means that they are more likely to talk about their thoughts and concerns. If something negative comes up that they struggle with, they are more likely to seek help, especially because they will know that it is okay to talk about such things.

CHAPTER SEVEN

For Parents

Parents, this is where you come in. You know your kids extremely well, often better than they know themselves. Discerning what is normal and what is pathologic can be difficult, but it starts with a loving, nonjudgmental, and sincere conversation with your child about what you see happening.

There are two key concepts to remember: **1) *love* and support your child, and 2) work on open *communication*.**[1] These conversations can be tough, and many teenagers simply don't want to talk about mental health or even realize how much they are struggling, but they need you. Listening completely and lovingly, even if it is hard for you to hear, is critical to helping your child. Receive their vulnerability in an accepting way. Most teenagers take their communication cues

---

1. I'm going to mention these *a lot* so get ready.

from their parents, so if you are closed off, embarrassed, or ashamed, they are more likely to reciprocate those things. This isn't a problem that you can always solve, but your child needs your help through the healing process.

I know this is hard. No one wants to see their child suffer, especially when we feel helpless to do anything about it. But you can do this. You love your child, so that part isn't hard. Knowing what to do is hard, but God is with you.

One important thing to remember is that *depression is more than just sadness* and *anxiety is more than just being nervous*. There are so many other elements that go along with them.[2] Understanding these other symptoms of guilt, worthlessness, loss of desire to engage in activities that they've enjoyed before, irritability, etc. helps you better understand what your child is going through. Watch for any changes from their baseline, especially their school performance or interactions with others. Random and non-specific aches and pains may pop up. They often don't know how to communicate what they are experiencing, so watching for some of the common signs is crucial.

Here are some general dos and don'ts to help show love and accomplishing open communication. There is more specific direction within each relevant chapter.

Dos:

▷ **Seek the Spirit** in all that you do. Seek for personal revelation to best understand how you can help your child.[3]

---

2. I'd encourage you to read the rest of the book to get a better understanding of these issues.

3. Doctrine and Covenants 100:2, 5–6

God loves them too[4] and wants the best for them. Let Him guide you and your teenager.

▷ Make sure your child knows *you* love them. Tell them both with your words and actions. Support and love are what they need most.

▷ *Communication* is a huge key to helping them. Poor communication or a perceived lack of love lead to a worsening stigma around the dangers of mental illness, which can then contribute to poorer communication. Show validation of their feelings more than focusing on the specific content of their struggles. Noah, the teenager who nearly took his own life, gave some great advice: "Talk to your kids; check up on them. It doesn't have to be a heart-to-heart, just talk about whatever, how their day was and other things." Just talk to them.

▷ *Help them understand* what they're feeling. Many teenagers lack the ability to understand what's going on inside them, and might read into things that aren't real. The Spirit can help guide you and your family to understand "things as they really are."[5]

▷ *Be honest*. Most of the time, we don't know what to do in these situations. It's okay to admit that to your child. Make it clear that you're on the journey towards healing and health together, even if you don't have all the answers.

▷ *Trust your child* enough to allow them to speak with their doctor and therapist alone. Give them a chance to experience some independence along their therapeutic journey.

▷ *Be open to advice* from others about how you can more effectively communicate with your child and about your choice of words. Kelly Furr, a Marriage and Family Thera-

---

4. Ask your kids what "Broken Record #1" is in this book.
5. Jacob 4:13; Doctrine and Covenants 79:2; Doctrine and Covenants 39:6

pist mentioned in chapter one, focuses a lot on this with parents: "Be reflective on 'Is how I'm interacting with my child affecting what is happening, and is there something I can do differently that might help?'" That's not criticism, but a way to move forward.

▷ *Respond lovingly to your child, don't react negatively.* There is a difference between *responses* and *reactions. Reactions* do not require thought, tend to be negative, and are more about what the listener believes. *Responding* requires seeing the bigger picture by focusing on the end goal instead of that moment. It's about true listening and showing the other person that you care about them. One of the biggest reasons for a lack of communication between teenagers and their parents is the child's worry about their parents' reaction to what they say.

▷ Be *gentle but persistent* in engaging with your teen. Be respectful if they don't want to talk, but don't stop trying. As I'm sure you've experienced, many teenagers struggle to communicate and some just simply don't try. Keep reaching out, even if you keep hitting roadblocks.

▷ *Seek help for yourself* as well. Self-care means different things to different people. Make sure to find time for yourself and do something that fills you up. This benefits *both* you and your child. Also be willing to participate in therapy. Individual therapy for you, as well as family therapy together, can do wonders to assist your child.

Don'ts:

▷ *Don't make your child feel ashamed or embarrassed* about their experience. Even though we want to think that our kids are completely unique, mental illness is very common, and is thus not worth worrying about what others might think. There is simply no need for shame or embarrassment.[6] Support and love are what they need most.

▷ *Don't minimize their experience.* While it is obviously important to recognize and feel gratitude for the blessings we have—things definitely could be worse—focusing on this initially can be counterproductive. Consistently emphasizing these points can send the message that your child's difficulties don't matter.

▷ *Don't overtly compare* them to their siblings or others. Any sort of "Why can't you be more like your sister?" or other such thoughts can be very hurtful, whether it's related to emotional struggles or other topics. Let them know you don't love them any less because of their difficulties.

▷ *Don't use language that could make your child think that they are something wrong that needs to be "fixed."* They are not defined by their struggles or mental illness. Treat them like a person instead of a disease.

▷ *Don't make the situation about you.* Kids today face challenges and pressures that we adults cannot fully understand; it is a different world from when we grew up (even if we're not that old). Sabotaging the discussion to make it about your problems is not okay. Avoid stating things like "When I was your age . . ." in a negative tone—it just makes things worse. Just like the bullet above about avoiding comparing your child to their siblings, don't compare them to you. This is about what *they* are going through.

Remember: *love and communication* **are the most important keys here.**

△▽ ▽ △▽

---

6. Ask your child about Broken Record #2.

James's story from chapter five on OCD tells us something important about understanding our kids' mental health: whether intentionally or inadvertently, we sometimes do things that contribute to their problems. It can be as severe as alcoholism or abuse, but it often shows up in more subtle ways. Maybe we just say the wrong thing, minimize their experiences, or don't show our love and appreciation for them in a way that they see and understand. As mentioned multiple times already, our job is to *love and communicate*. If you need your child, a therapist, or another professional to point out ways you can improve what you say and do, be open to it. This isn't about blame or shaming or anything other than helping your child and you function in life as well as possible.

James's experience also shows us that the effects of mental illness, whether from OCD or another diagnosis, can be very debilitating spiritually. We have discussed how mental illness can lead to a loss of feeling the Spirit, but that can subsequently lead one to give up on their relationship with Christ. Everyone deals with their trials and problems differently, and this causes some people to follow a different path. While we certainly want our loved ones to make and keep sacred covenants, trying to force them into spiritual or religious practices when they are in the throes of a mental illness may not be the most productive way to address the situation. Again, this is where seeking revelation through the Spirit can help guide you to know the best way to address these matters with your child.

△▽ △▽ △▽

Prayers to relieve the struggles of our children are not always answered in the way we want them to. We are supposed to struggle in this life, even though it may break our heart to see our children suffer. Seek revelation for insight and guidance on helping them through their darkness. Lisa Gauchay, the therapist in Salt Lake City mentioned previously, advised, "With the youth, we need to witness their losses more and help them hold it without trying to fix it." Taking away their difficulties doesn't allow them to progress emotionally or spiritually. Kelly Furr adds that "Heavenly Father felt like it was important for us to have this wide range of emotions, so we shouldn't just try to get rid of them, but figure out how to manage them."[7] **Remember: love is the most important thing**. God does not take away our trials, but He does walk through them with us; that is what we should do with our kids, as well.

A priesthood leader once advised me that God does not make mistakes. I believe this completely. It's not a mistake that we are here in this circumstance. That doesn't make it ideal, fun, or any less difficult, but God allows us to suffer in this life so as to become more like Him. We should, therefore, not feel ashamed or embarrassed that our child or family is suffering with a mental or emotional affliction. None of us are perfect, but *our lack of perfection does not shut God out of our lives*. Seek Him always!

Another piece of advice from many therapists is to re-connect with your purpose. This can include your spiritual purpose as a child of God, your temporal purpose in raising your kid(s), or any other purpose in life that you have found. Getting back to the basics in your own and your child's life can do wonders to bring an appropriate perspective as you work together and with God.

I mentioned this earlier, but it is important that we as parents are open to growth. There are ways in which we can do

---

7. Both of these quotes sound a lot like Broken Record #3, don't they? (If you haven't read the other parts of this book, ask your child what Broken Record #3 is.)

more to support our children, ways that we don't even recognize currently. And it's okay to have a therapist or other professional point this out. This does not mean you are a bad parent! If you tell and show your child that you love them, then you qualify as a good parent.

All in all, allow yourself some grace, because Jesus does. Don't beat yourself up for not being perfect, but learn to "trust His grace"[8] in your life. You deserve that.

Jennifer is Katie's mother whom we met in chapter three. Understandably, she has struggled with coming to terms with her daughter's anxiety and knowing how best to deal with it. Nathan, another teenager with anxiety, and Jennifer both offer some wonderful advice.

1. **Communication**   "I can now say she's dealing with anxiety, and I think for a long time I wasn't able to admit that. But it really helps when you can just be honest about it and talk about it. Sadly, we [as a society] don't." She has found strength in being open with her daughter, with her other kids, her husband, and other people she can trust. She has found some benefit in being open about it with Katie's friends' parents when staying at their house, other family members, and schoolteachers. While we might run the risk of over sharing our problems, Jennifer only shares it in circumstances in which it's necessary to support Katie.

2. **Family**   Jennifer describes the absolute necessity of focusing on your relationship with your spouse or partner: "We need to debrief and end the night together. Sometimes parents choose their kids over each other, and I

---

8. "Sweet Hour of Prayer," LDS Hymnbook

don't think that's healthy. Communicating with your spouse, putting your marriage first, working together to help your child. I could see how couples who have a child with lots of health issues could definitely grow apart."

3. **Trust** Nathan, the teenager above who admits that his anxiety has led him to lie to his parents to avoid certain situations that cause him stress, has experienced this broken trust with his parents. He knows he has been the biggest contributor to the trust issues with his parents, but part of it comes from the differing relationships he has with his mom and dad. "I communicate well with my mom, not as much with my dad." He is working to rebuild the trust as best as he can, though it's certainly not a quick process. Recognizing and accepting that sometimes others have a better connection with your child while you continue to work on your relationship with them can help them progress in addressing their struggles.

4. **Encouragement** Possibly the most difficult thing about supporting someone with a mental illness can be knowing when to push them to do needed things and when to back off. Unfortunately, there is no simple answer to this. "That's the hardest part," said Jennifer. "Am I too hard on her? Am I too easy on her? Is this going to hurt her down the road because I let her off too easily?" She recommends seeking the guidance of the Spirit and following your parenting intuition, but it takes time to figure out what works for you and your child. "I'm sure I've done it wrong multiple times—pushed her when I shouldn't have—but you learn as you go."

Jennifer has also tried laying out the different options in the situation for Katie. She sometimes has to clarify that "all of these options are uncomfortable, but you have to choose one." She also has tried to focus on the most important matter in the situation. For example, if your child is struggling in the moment, it is better to help them calm down and get to school late than to force them there on time in a bad state of mind. Don't let perfection be the enemy of good.

Pushing too hard in some circumstances can cause a lot of trouble, but not pushing enough can feed an avoidance pattern in your child. As we talked about above, be gentle yet persistent. You will not get it right every time, and that's okay. Do the best you can. Seek the Spirit to help you. There is no overarching answer, but like I said before, allow yourself some grace. Focus on *love and communication*, and God will bless you.

5. **Treatment**   Jennifer mentioned her strong desire to get Katie the proper treatment for her anxiety. "I don't want her to get to be 20 and have us say, 'Wow, we really could have enjoyed her teenage years better if she had been on medication.'" The Lord blesses us with so many tools to have our prayers answered; one of which is the blessing of scientific discovery. Many people view medication as something to be avoided at all costs, and while there can be down sides to taking prescribed medicine, the potential upsides for people who are struggling are huge and cannot be quantified. Sometimes medication is part of the answer to our prayers.

6. **Role of Willpower**   Never suggest that the problem is because of a lack of willpower. Elder Alexander B. Morrison stated in *Valley of Sorrow*, "Anyone who has ever witnessed the incredible, well-nigh unbearable pain of a severe panic attack knows full well that *nobody* would suffer that way if all that was needed was to show a little willpower." That

goes for all different mental illnesses, not just panic at-tacks; it truly is suffering. No one would choose it. If will-power is all it took, then mental illness would be nearly non-existent.

◿▽ ◿▽ ◿▽

The underlying message you should know is that you can do this. Your teenager needs your love and support more than anything. Just sitting and being with them is often all it takes. You can't take away all the suffering, but you can help them cope with it. ***God loves you and your family. Never* forget that!** He understands because He deals with this as a parent all the time. Let Him help you. I wish you and your family strength in your trials and all the blessings eternity can offer.

CHAPTER EIGHT

Where to Turn for Help

There have been lots of times when various aspects of being a member of The Church of Jesus Christ of Latter-day Saints has negatively affected my mental health. There have also been lots of times when it has been beneficial and positive for my mental health. The vast majority of times when it was a negative for me it was because of the culture of the church members, not from the church or Gospel of Christ itself. That is why I wrote this book. There is a lot of misunderstanding by members of the church about what mental illness is and how it fits into our belief system. Teenagers are often the ones hit hardest by the misconceptions.

When I have focused on the love Jesus offers all of us, that is when being a member of this church and a follower of Christ has helped me with my mental and emotional issues. Choose to focus on Him and not on what others may or may not think. We are eternal beings that will be around forever, and putting too much emphasis on what others think right now does not help us.

I have been in extremely dark emotional depths with my depression and anxiety. The process of training to become a physician is very grueling and has caused some lasting emotional scars. I still require medication, therapy, and coping skills to keep going. But I also live a happy life. I have many wonderful blessings, and God helps me through every day.

But it's easy to be mad at God when things aren't going right. I have been through episodes of anger at heaven, as have millions of others. It is often hard to remember that our problems actually help us out and "shall be for [our] good."[1] Allow yourself to feel tough emotions and to embrace hard things. God is with you, *especially* in the hard times; let Him in. Allow yourself to be healed, even if you aren't cured.

Make sure to create some healthy coping skills for yourself. What can you do when things get tough that help you? For example, I like to do jigsaw puzzles. It calms me and gives me a way to create something out of chaos, both in the physical world and in my mental world. That is one of my coping skills.

Don't just come up with one coping skill; come up with multiple. Many people use exercise as a coping skill, which is excellent! But what happens if you have an injury and can no longer do the exercise? Suddenly your only coping skill is gone. Find multiple things, both big and small, that help you cope. Develop some that are physical (e.g., exercise), some that are spiritual (e.g., scripture reading, temple attendance, mindfulness), and some that are mental (e.g., reading or painting). Make sure some involve connecting with other people.[2] And make sure some of them are simple and don't require a lot of time. Develop these coping skills intentionally.

---

1. Doctrine and Covenants 122:7
2. Not through a screen, but actually in-person. I know, I know.

What is the story you tell about yourself? Is it a negative one about how "broken" you may be emotionally? How you are worthless and it would be better for everyone if you weren't around anymore? That you can't perform at your full capacity because you have a mental disorder that holds you back? Or is it the story Jesus tells about you? He tells a story of you as a beloved child of the Almighty God of the Universe, someone who is destined to become a God yourself, who will receive a crown of glory in the wide expanse of Celestial eternities through the atonement of Jesus Christ? A story where you are someone who can overcome, no matter how hard it may be, because you are willing to utilize the tools He provides for you? Someone who is not afraid to call upon the powers of Heaven to achieve your best self? Life can be tough, but it can also be wonderful. If you remember nothing else from this book, remember Broken Record #1: **God always loves you!** No matter how broken we may be, we can't escape His love.

Allow yourself some grace, because Jesus does.

COMMON CONCERN

◁   You hear a lot about seeking help if you need it, but maybe more important is allowing others to help. When a family member or friend sincerely asks if you are doing okay, or that they're worried about you, talking with them about your struggles is the first step to addressing your illness. It can be daunting to approach others on your own and discuss your feelings, but those opportunities often come to you in the form of others. This is one of God's ways of telling you that He loves you,[3] and I strongly encourage you to open up when others invite you in!

---

3. Broken Record #1! Broken Record #1! It's like you're on a game show and keep winning!

Bibliography

Alexander B. Morrison. *Valley of Sorrow*. Deseret Book Company. 2003. Page 23, 26.

Alexander B. Morrison. "Myths about mental illness." Ensign. The Church of Jesus Christ of Latter-day Saints. October 2005. Accessed online: https://www.churchofjesuschrist.org/study/ensign/2005/10/myths-about-mental-illness

American Psychiatric Association. *Diagnostic and statistical manual of mental disorders* (5th ed.). 2015.

Cecil O. Samuelson. "What does it mean to be perfect." *New Era*. The Church of Jesus Christ of Latter-day Saints." January 2006. Accessed online: https://www.churchofjesuschrist.org/study/new-era/2006/01/what-does-it-mean-to-be-perfect

Dale G. Renlund. "Experience God's love." Brigham Young University Devotional. 3 December 2019. Published online: https://speeches.byu.edu/talks/dale-g-renlund/experience-gods-love/

Dale G. Renlund. "Understanding Suicide." Video, The Church of Jesus Christ of Latter-day Saints. Published online:

https://www.churchofjesuschrist.org/media/video/2018-06-0020-renlund-understanding-suicide

James E. Talmage. *Jesus the Christ*. Missionary Reference Library, Deseret Book Company. 1983. p. 345–46.

Jeffrey R. Holland. "Like a broken vessel." *Ensign*. The Church of Jesus Christ of Latter-day Saints. November 2013. Accessed online: https://www.churchofjesuschrist.org/study/general-conference/2013/10/like-a-broken-vessel

Joseph Smith. "The Great Jehovah." *Ensign*. The Church of Jesus Christ of Latter-day Saints. June 1994. Accessed online: https://www.churchofjesuschrist.org/study/ensign/1994/06/the-great-jehovah

Katie Lambert. "What the church has said about suicide: comforting answers from church leaders." *LDS Living*. 15 May 2018. Published exclusively online: https://www.ldsliving.com/what-the-church-has-said-about-suicide-comforting-answers-from-church-leaders/s/88292

Lucy W. Smith as related to Bishop K. J. Fetzer and contained in a letter from Bishop Fetzer to the Smith children, August 7, 1953, *Smith Papers*, box 151, fd. 3. As cited in article from Mary Jane Woodger.

M. Russell Ballard. "Suicide: some things we know, and some we do not." *Ensign*. The Church of Jesus Christ of Latter-day Saints. October 1987. Accessed online: https://www.churchofjesuschrist.org/study/ensign/1987/10/suicide-some-things-we-know-and-some-we-do-not

Mary Jane Woodger. "Cheat the asylum of a victim: George Albert Smith's 1909–12 breakdown." *Journal of Mormon History*. 2008. 34(4):113–152.

Medline Plus. National Institutes of Health, US National Library of Medicine. Accessed online: https://medlineplus.gov/teenmentalhealth.html

Mental Health website. The Church of Jesus Christ of Latter-day Saints. https://mentalhealth.churchofjesuschrist.org

Michael Hirsch, Robert J. Birnbaum. "Selective serotonin re-uptake inhibitors: Pharmacology, administration, and side effects." Wolters Kluwer. March 2020. Published exclusively online: https://www.uptodate.com/contents/selective-serotonin-reuptake-inhibitors-pharmacology-administration-and-side-effects

Regine Galanti. "How to cope with teen anxiety." *Psyche.* 3 March 2021. Published exclusively online: https://psyche.co/guides/how-to-cope-with-teen-anxiety-using-techniques-from-cbt

Sheri L. Dew. *Go Forward with Faith: The Biography of Gordon B. Hinckley.* Deseret Book Company. 1996. pp. 382, 384.

William W. Walford, William B. Bradbury. "Sweet Hour of Prayer." *Hymns,* The Church of Jesus Christ of Latter-day Saints. 1985.

DR. KYLE BRADFORD JONES is an Associate Clinical Professor in Family and Preventive Medicine at the University of Utah, School of Medicine. He grew up in Farmington, Utah, and attended school at both Utah State University and the Medical College of Wisconsin after serving in the Ukraine Kiev Mission. He completed residency in Family Medicine at the University of Utah in 2012. He is the author of the award-winning book *Fallible: A Memoir of a Young Physician's Struggle with Mental Illness*, and is passionate about working to decrease the stigma of mental illness. He lives in Holladay, Utah with his wonderful wife and four great kids.